Be Creative

The Toolkit for Business Success

Be Creative

The Toolkit
for Business Success

Neil Coade

INTERNATIONAL THOMSON BUSINESS PRESS
I(T)P® **An International Thomson Publishing Company**

London • Bonn • Boston • Johannesburg • Madrid • Melbourne • Mexico City • New York • Paris
Singapore • Tokyo • Toronto • Albany, NY • Belmont, CA • Cincinnati, OH • Detroit, MI

To my inspiration,
Sandra and Sam.

First edition 1997

Typeset by LaserScript Limited, Mitcham, Surrey
Printed in the UK by TJ International Ltd, Cornwall

ISBN 1–86152087–5

International Thomson Business Press   International Thomson Business Press
Berkshire House   20 Park Plaza
168–173 High Holborn   13th Floor
London WC1V 7AA   Boston MA 02116
UK   USA

http:\\www.itbp.com

Contents

List of figures

List of tables

Preface

This book will examine some of the problems of being creative in a turbulent business environment, developing a creative corporate environment, seeking business development opportunities, selecting and developing creative people, rewarding creative activity and preventing your company from creative stagnation. A broad definition of creativity could be the starting-point of the process of innovation and can be defined as bringing into existence a product or service which is the product of imaginative thinking. Innovation is the management process that supports creativity, and can be defined as the successful use or exploitation of new ideas and the crucial link between creativity and innovation that turns the most bizarre ideas into new products and services. My definition of creativity would centre on the need for managers to take an objective view of a situation and initiate and utilize new thinking to develop new products, services and management systems.

I would encourage you to develop your own view of creativity and innovation and how they apply to your organization. Your organization may employ 500 or 50,000 people, so the need to tailor some of the approaches, models and exercises to the specific needs of your organization is paramount. You need to consider some of the following questions to start opening your mind to the key issues concerning creativity and innovation:

- Does your company have an innovation strategy?

- How do you monitor the competitive threat from new companies?

- Do customers recognize your company as creative?

- Do you actively recruit creative people?

- Have you read the corporate training and development strategy and does it recognize creativity as a key skill competency?

- Do you reward people in a creative manner?

- How do you expect to prevent your company from suffering from creative stagnation?

- Do you have your own business development programme?

My teaching and consultancy experience in innovation and creativity has focused my attention on the fact that there is a lack of publications that concentrate the reader on the vital role played by people in the creative process within companies and on the business benefits to be achieved if the whole process of creativity could be more effectively managed. This book is focused on the strategic planner who is emerging from a battle-scarred business environment and searching for some assistance in understanding and taking advantage of the business opportunities that lie ahead.[1]

I would like to discuss this book in an informal manner and to tell you why it has been written. In reviewing innovation and creativity issues with existing and potential managers it has become clear to me that no single book tackles head-on the issues of people management and the competitive advantage that can develop from their successful management. There are some texts which deal with innovation strategy, managing change, creative marketing and the new product development process, but nothing that puts forward a straightforward argument for increased focus on people and their link with successful creativity and strategic planning. I will treat the reader as someone who craves new thinking and innovation in their organization and who recognizes that the successful management of people might help them to develop a strategic response to the lack of creative drive within the company. I will assist you in your thinking and hopefully simplify the processes and systems which your company uses to promote innovation and provide you with a blueprint that can be used to start the creative snowball rolling.

This book will enable you to:

- understand the key elements underpinning successful creativity and innovation;

- influence the corporate strategy of your business;

- effectively construct a dynamic corporate environment to enhance creativity and innovation;

- design an organizational and management strategy which can respond to the changing needs of the customer and the marketplace;

- enable you to influence the process and systems that develop and recruit creative people;

- help you to explore the options available for rewarding the business developers of the future.

I will apply a degree of clarity to the discussion of creativity and focus your mind away from the two extremes of, say, discussing the development of Concorde and the merits of a company suggestion scheme. This book has a practical focus and it contains a series of exercises that will assist you in thinking about the decision-making processes needed for successful creativity. The book will centre on some of the problems experienced by companies and managers in their attempts to introduce some of these concepts and ideas and it will discuss the difficulties involved in seizing new business opportunities. The book will be interactive and will allow you to experiment with some of my ideas before you present them to the other managers within your company.

Creativity is now being recognized by senior managers as a necessary competence for the next millennium, although it is still considered a haphazard process. When senior managers are asked to discuss the subject of innovation and creativity, they will tend to focus on the major technological advances that have been made by their organizations or the famous successes such as the UK/French joint venture which developed the Concorde passenger plane. The 'big idea' still seems to catch and hold the attention of senior management, rather than the gradual improvement in management, service, product or systems which may provide consistent improvement for the average company.

The underlying philosophy of the book is that business people are being asked to boost company performance and that the creative efforts of people are at the centre of the challenge. This book has been written for three types of business people:

1   Experienced business people who are enjoying an unexpected increase in business activity through their creative or innovative efforts.

2   People who are undertaking business management programmes and expecting their roles within the company to become increasingly oriented towards creating new business through innovative practices.

3   Teachers of management who may find the structure of the book useful as a teaching aid to practical exercises that may be conducted as part of a strategy workshop or a distance-learning programme.

'Business' is an all-encompassing term which could be applied to the retail sector as well as manufacturing or financial services. In addition, the term 'product' is used generically and it includes services. Creativity is a difficult concept to define and is often described as the association of ideas that would normally not have been put together. It goes out of the normal pattern of the mind. It is lateral thinking, which is logical, analytical and follows a chain of reasoning. The argument is that if a clear application of creativity can take place, innovation will be the outcome. Innovation is the implementation of a new concept which is different from existing ideas and has a series of corporate and customer benefits attached. Creativity can also be viewed as a process of finding new problems to evaluate, finding new ways of solving the problem and, as a result, using the best way to solve the problem.

We will focus on the creative process and divide it into seven stages:

1   Orientation: pointing out the problem.

2   Preparation: gathering pertinent data.

3   Analysis: breaking down the relevant material.

4   Idea-generation: building idea alternatives.

5   Incubation: letting the idea grow to allow illumination.

6   Synthesis: putting the pieces together.

7   Evaluation: judging the resulting ideas.

This process needs to be kept in mind while you are reading this book. It will help you understand the process of creativity and the fact that your company and its employees will be at different stages of the process at different times when new ideas are being considered.

I wish to thank Steven Reed, the commissioning editor, who provided me with the opportunity to write this book, and I also wish to thank Linda Yelverton of International Thomson Publishing for her continued assistance during the preparation of the initial and final manuscripts.

I would also like to extend my thanks to the individuals from a collection of companies who have allowed me to discuss creativity and innovation issues with them, including 3M, ICL Fujitsu, Agfa, Rank Xerox, Leo Burnett, Imagination and British Gas.

The love and encouragement of my wife Sandra and Sam my little boy have been a source of creativity for me throughout the writing of this book.

I would like to open this book and complete my introduction by using a quote from a leading consultant in the area of creative thinking, Simon Majaro:

You cannot expect to be creative if you do not take lunch.

The interpretation of the quote is that you need to give yourself thinking time in every working day, otherwise you will find it difficult to generate ideas and to allow them to incubate and become productive concepts to be used in your company.

How to use this book

This book will be based on what is already working in creative companies and will draw on my experience/research with companies which are actively involved in new innovation and creative practices. It is structured around seven chapters and the main objective is to assist you in answering some of the issues that face your business:

- Do you understand the key elements underpinning successful creativity and innovation in your company?

- Can you influence the corporate strategy of your business through creativity?

- How can you effectively construct a dynamic corporate environment to enhance creativity and innovation?

- What are the key aspects of designing an organizational and management strategy which can respond to the changing needs of the customer and the marketplace?

- How can you develop systems which recruit, reward and motivate the business developers of tomorrow?

These questions should be at the forefront of your mind when you are reading this book. The techniques I will outline will assist you in preparing your organization to meet some of the challenges of the future. You can expect a clear and concise understanding of the issues and potential rewards of exploring the development of a strategy for creativity through people. You will interact with the book, which will use a series of modern examples of successful activities already being used by existing companies. The structure of this book is illustrated by the model in Figure 0.1.

The book will provide readers with an easily accessible and constructive method of approaching the challenge of innovation and creativity, enabling them to develop a successful strategy and maintain a competitive advantage. During the establishment of a creative corporate environment the reader/manager needs to deploy a variety of skills: analysis and understanding of the need for creativity, environmental awareness, strategy formulation and implementation, and a clear knowledge of the creative competencies of the existing business. These skills will be fully explored in this text.

FIGURE 0.1 The main factors for success in strategic creativity through people

TABLE 0.1 Structure and themes of the book

Chapter	*Levels of understanding/reader skills*
1 Introduction	Explanation of strategic creativity.
2 The creative corporate environment	Awareness of the main factors affecting the creative business environment. This chapter will include a series of exercises which assist readers to assess their corporate environment and determine their position. It will also enable the reader to compare aspects of the company environment which threaten the creative success of the business.
3 Innovation and the opportunities for the strategic planner	This chapter will discuss the design of systems which can assist in the identification and exploitation of business opportunites through people.
4 Selection of creative people	The selection concepts to be considered in building creative organizations. The criteria on which to select a variety of organizational settings.
5 Developing creative people	The importance of strategic planning in the process and the need for a clear competitive analysis. A model of the competitive advantage that can be gained by a creative company.
6 Rewarding creative activity	The variety of options open to the creative organization. The advantages and disadvantages of particular approaches.
7 Preventing organizational stagnation	Introduces new human resource strategies to prevent organizational stagnation. A simple model to address the organizational issues to consider prior to the design of an appropriate structure/systems as a starting-point for the strategic planner.

There are many books on new product development which tend to specialize in new product development processes and there are some books which specialize in innovation strategy. Also, there are many books on change management in organizations. This book offers a clear difference from previous publications because of its practical nature and its emphasis on taking the business person through the actual problems involved in seizing business opportunities in a new and innovative way through the creative efforts of people.

The structure and themes of the book are illustrated in Table 0.1 and will provide the reader with an easily accessible and constructive method of assessing the competencies required to develop an innovative approach to managing creative people. During the discovery stage the strategic planner needs to deploy a range of skills and techniques.

This book is based on what works in practice, and many of the ideas have already been developed through my teaching on management development programmes in creativity and innovation and my research interests.

Neil Coade
London, 1997

■ **CHAPTER ONE** ■

Introduction: strategic creativity

Creativity is the starting-point for successful innovation and therefore needs to be nurtured and developed by the strategic planners within a company. It is fundamental to the success of organizations because it provides the basis for the development of new thinking and the generation of ideas. The creative process is evident in a whole series of organizations from government agencies, the health sector, manufacturing concerns, design consultancies and computer software developers.

Creativity can be seen in the large American multinationals, Japanese global companies and UK start-up businesses. It is not restricted to the household names that we see advertising products and services on our television screens every day. It may involve the development of a new set of ideas for improvement of a management system which revolutionalizes performance or customer service. Alternatively, it could include the introduction of new thinking around a technological advance which has a major impact on the development of a product and the structure of a market.

My definition of creativity is the bringing into existence of a product or service which is the outcome of imaginative thinking. Imagination can be defined as being 'mental faculty forming images or concepts of objects not existent or present, creative faculty of the mind'. An objective viewpoint is needed, allied with initiative and the turning of new thinking into something useful and real.[1]

If creativity is the starting-point, then innovation is the process that enables imaginative thinking to become a reality. Innovation has been defined by the Department of Trade & Industry in the United Kingdom as the successful exploitation of new ideas, and this definition seems to capture the very essence of innovation.

The emphasis on thinking is important because people require time to think and this resource is in very short supply in many companies. The effective use of time, as well as the ability to develop new thinking, is at the heart of the challenge facing many companies in their search for creative solutions to problems. The focus of creativity is shown in Figure 1.1.

FIGURE 1.1   The focus of creativity

Independent research

An independent research programme undertaken by the author has produced some interesting results. The research was based on a series of questions which explored the definition of creativity, the problems associated with managing creative outcomes and the difficulties in introducing a corporate culture and strategy that can assist the creative process. The research interviews were conducted informally and used a diverse sample of people including advertising executives, training specialists, entrepreneurs, computer software engineers, human resource directors, product and business development executives, managing directors and sales managers of a variety of small, medium-sized and large companies.

One of the key questions the participants were asked referred to their understanding of the definition of creativity, and surprisingly there was very little uniformity in their answers. The problem would seem to be that the creative process is often closely linked to individuals and their behaviour within different organizations. One of the major problems that was highlighted by the research was the need for a set of focus points which could be used by the strategic planner within a company to design the foundations of an effective strategy to achieve high levels of creativity and eventually innovation. Certainly the broad view of creativity taken in this book centres on the need for new thinking and the search for new ways of applying that thinking to the business development opportunities that are offered in the marketplace. The research outcomes produced a series of focus points that can be used to start thinking about the strategic benefits of integrating creativity into the strategic processes in your company.

The research outcomes centred on the following factors:

1   *Objectivity*: the need for objectivity is important when considering new creative ideas in companies and this was fully recognized by all the respondents involved in the research. The ability to examine facts, ideas, markets and customer reaction without colouring the customer's views by feelings or biased opinions was seen as a fundamental prerequisite for success in the search for creativity.

2   *Challenging perceived thinking*: the benefit of challenging established thinking was recognized by the research sample as a fundamental way of re-examining the old methods used by the company and developing a springboard for future action.

3   *Nurturing curiosity*: it is important to foster the ability to promote a climate where the creative people in the company are very receptive to the need to discover new methods, products or services and to implement them successfully.

4   *Changing mind sets*: another finding was that the changing of employee mind sets was being used as a method of encouraging people to think laterally. This was supported by education programmes aimed at teaching employees that logical analysis is important and is the basis of effective creativity. These organizations were gaining support for creativity by changing employee mind sets from a defensive attitude towards creativity to a positive attitude. This assisted the development of a creative corporate environment.

5   *Process of problem-solving*: new methods of problem-solving are being used by the sample to encourage an open approach to the discovery of appropriate solutions. Problem-solving techniques are being used that stress listening, protecting ideas from initial criticism, elimination of status, supporting uncertainty, learning from mistakes and, overall, a belief in helping employee ideas find expression within the company.

6   *Establishing a flow of ideas*: identify the most effective tools and techniques for harnessing the creative potential of people and facilitating the generation of ideas and explore the differences between individual, small group and corporate idea-generation systems. The key objective in many of the companies involved in

the research was to assist the employees of the company in their individual search to find expression for their ideas and corporate projects.

7   *Measured risk-taking*: the ability to take measured risks is promoted by many companies in the research sample and this started with the predisposition of managers towards risk-taking being re-examined and focused on the positive need for risk-taking in the company. The rewards received by some employees were geared towards the open desire of senior management to see experimentation and measured risks taking place throughout the company.

8   *Ability to question not solve*: the research sample showed a strong need for the open examination and questioning of the traditional concepts and ideas being used in each company. The emphasis was placed not on always finding a solution but on the institutionalization of the process of questioning methods and procedures – or, as it was stated by one senior executive, 'engendering a restlessness throughout the corporate environment'.

9   *Freedom to act*: the freedom to take decisions which support the achievement of the company vision – which is focused on the need for creativity and innovation – was seen as vital by the research sample. The ability to generate decision options was viewed throughout these companies as a skill that it was necessary to acquire. This has to be complemented by the ability rationally to evaluate a series of ideas against an emerging and volatile business environment.

EXERCISE 1: What does creativity mean in your organization?

Consider your own company: examine the research outcomes outlined on the preceding pages and think about the methods your company utilizes to manage creativity.

1   Outline the key outcomes of your company's strategy for creativity:

2   What level of objectivity is exercised when ideas are being considered?

- low level;

- medium level;

- high level.

3   Identify the programmes within the company that are actively changing employee mind sets:

4   Identify which actions need to be taken to improve the flow of ideas:

EXERCISE REVIEW

You may find that your thinking focused on specific procedures or systems used in the management of creativity within your company. Outline below what these are.

- idea-generation procedures:

- decision-making systems:

- training and development:

- problem-solving techniques:

> ■   freedom to express ideas:
>
>
>
> ■   company initiatives on changing mind sets:

The role of the strategic planner will change and you may find yourself becoming the discoverer of the emerging business strategies throughout the company. The role of the strategic planner is central to the creative activities of your management team, and the strategic planner can act as the catalyst for change who encourages creative strategic thinking throughout the top team of the company.

The role of the strategist will be to act as a strategic opportunist who seeks new ways of building creative teams, designing new corporate structures and suggesting new management styles that enable creative action to take place. The role of the strategist will be to identify exactly how to incorporate creativity into the company and develop a business strategy to maximize competitive advantage. The starting-point will be to clarify your corporate interpretation of creativity, highlight the key difference between creativity and innovation, and stress the need for both elements. The focus of your thinking will aim to place creativity among the key business drivers as a tool to achieve competitiveness. The view that creativity and innovation are haphazard is not strategic has to be strongly countered by the strategist. The organization of creativity can be assisted by the encouragement of networks of creative people and the introduction of new ideas on creativity and management into the company. Achieving a core competency in creativity is a key factor in building competitive advantage in the organization of the future.

The next phase of competitive advantage will lie in the corporate ability to develop a tailored approach to the creative process, one that suits the way your company operates and will allow you to build an element of sustainability into your creative abilities. Many companies have focused on the need to develop competitive advantage through new corporate structures, economies of scale, business re-engineering and new planning systems. The effective management of people is one factor which has been neglected in the past. The link between creativity, people and competitive advantage is often left to chance by many companies. The promotion of creativity and innovation within a formal framework will be your overall objective, and the redesign of the corporate vision and mission statement to position creativity at the heart of the business will be your first task. This needs to be pre-empted by a determined and wide-ranging re-evaluation of your company position within the business environment and of the strategic parameters in which to locate your corporate efforts in creativity and innovation.

Competitive advantage through creativity is being explored by a range of companies, including 3M, Rank Xerox and ICL Fujitsu. The approaches being tried vary considerably but they seem to have a common theme, which is the linking of creative people to the business development activities of the company and consequently the future success of the business.

Pressures on companies to manage creativity successfully

The pressures on companies to manage creativity are immense. There is a clear need to plan the creative process as effectively as possible and this can only be achieved by understanding the marketplace in some detail. The strategist will need to ensure that the resources of the company are a successful match for the available opportunities in the market. The pressure is on companies to develop new channels to reach their customers and to manage the process by developing strategies that secure success. These strategies must be supported by a detailed understanding of customer behaviour, which should be incorporated into the creative process. These are some of the pressures that you will have to manage to ensure that creativity becomes a key driver in the constant search for corporate success:

- *Customer behaviour*: the key factors influencing the behaviour of customers are the range of choice now open to customers and the fact that the level of choice is increasing all the time.

- *Customization*: the demand for different, more specific and customized products and services is developing rapidly.

- *New economic environment*: the economic environment is placing pressure on organizations to be more creative in their search for ways of differentiating products/services from those of competitors.

- *Managing transition*: managing complex transitions is not restricted to any particular sector of the economy and affects all sectors, including computer software, car manufacturing, retailing, financial services, healthcare provision and marketing services.

- *High levels of quality*: customers are demanding the highest possible levels of quality and companies are being placed under pressure not only to get it right first time but also to be first in introducing product and service improvements – in many cases suggesting the quality improvements before the customer even expresses an interest in the improvements.

Difficult trading conditions leave many companies with a poor level of business confidence and a lack of understanding of the real nature of customer behaviour. New energy needs to be integrated into the operations of the business and a strategic revitalization is required. The reaction of many companies is to take the safe route and invest in recognized products and services which have a proven market and a established customer group. This approach can be beneficial, but as companies compete they have recognized that the active involvement of the customer leads to products and services that are more tailored to their specific needs. The profile of the customer is changing in many sectors and the ability to target the right customer group is increasingly important as resources become even more tightly managed.

The new ways of growing businesses are based on sustainable growth and acquisitive behaviour. Companies are building long-term strategies for business growth which underpin their creative efforts, and investing in new products and service development as a method of securing a competitive advantage in national and world markets. The new methods being developed by companies need to be concerned with long-term success and sustainable business development and not short-term acquisitive actions by companies. This requires a complete evaluation of the fundamental principles used by your company to develop new business, maximizing the contribution of marketing techniques to the identification of customer needs and appropriate business development strategies.

The business development strategy needs to take advantage of business opportunities as effectively as possible and the pressure will be on the creative organization to offer innovative solutions to customer requirements, accelerating the speed to market of new business development ideas by effectively planning, streamlining and managing your process of creativity and innovation. The pressure will be placed on you to manage the speed to market. It is important to get it right first time in terms of strategic management and implementation.

You may not know the answer to the question of how best to develop the creative strategy for your company but you may have the right questions to ask your top team. The questions being considered by you and many other strategic planners in creative companies include the following:

- Do we require a strategy for creativity/innovation in our company?

- What style of management needs to exist to support the creative process?

- How are we going to allow the creative individual to operate within a team and independently at the same time?

- Can our people meet the changing needs of the customer?

- Do we clearly understand those needs?

- How are the individual needs of customers changing?

Strategic people management

The drivers and coordinators of creativity will be the strategic planning and human resource specialists, who will need to build an ongoing partnership to enhance corporate creativity within the company. This process needs to be supported by effective analysis and development of the organizational skills of creativity, innovation and entrepreneurship.

The introduction of creative people management (highlighted in Figure 1.2) involves the acceptance of change as an integral part of the creative process within your company. The creative process cannot be left to its own devices; it has to be audited, checked and evaluated on a regular basis. It requires that strategic planning and the human resource strategist work in partnership to ensure an effective strategy for creativity is developed by the company.

Building the corporate competencies of the business is fundamental to the success of the innovative company. It is important to have a focus on the future which develops a strategy that can sustain creativity and innovation. The mission of the company needs to recognize that *everyone* can be creative if the opportunity to excel is provided by senior management. Creativity will become a prerequisite of continued employment in most companies: if you cannot be creative no one will employ you.

FIGURE 1.2 Creative people management

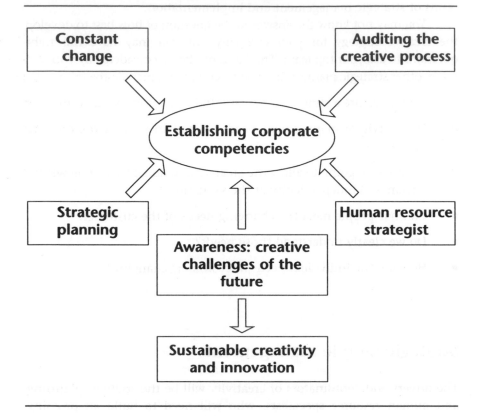

Influence on strategic planning

In this book strategy is taken to be a method of determining a sense of direction for a business. Determining the direction of the business involves understanding how the company is positioned against its competitors and within the business environment in order to achieve sustainable competitive advantage.

Core competencies are an integral part of the creative business strategy and can be described as the aspects of business operations that your company excels in or is simply very good at carrying out. These will include the following:

■ *People*: the effective management of people can focus on training and development which can concentrate on key business issues, such as new product development and improving the launch of new products within existing markets. The methods of internal selection can be centred on making the most of the appropriate skills available to particular areas of need within the business. The strategy for human resource management can also be geared towards providing a method of motivating and integrating the supplier organizations that support your business.

- *Operations*: a constant push is required towards improving each operational unit within the company. It will focus on raising standards and creating quality management or competitive benchmarking programmes which could be used to focus the attention of every company employee on the need consistently to improve operations.

- *Manufacturing*: world's-best manufacturing standards are met and then exceeded by the innovative company searching for a method of maintaining the pressures for competitive advantage. Corporate standards must be beaten, and the successful company will play a role in setting industry standards. New control methods can be used to promote high levels of manufacturing capability throughout the company.

- *Knowledge*: companies will need to build high levels of corporate knowledge through listening to the difficult and complex needs of their customers. This will help them to develop the benefits of partnership through working alongside their customer base to stay ahead in the technological race with their competitors.

- *Corporate structure*: it is important to design an organizational structure which is focused on your markets and to instil a dynamic orientation towards the customer throughout the company, so that you can develop an adaptive organizational structure that can meet the increased demands of your customer base.

Innovation and creativity can be added to this list of core competencies that companies are building to strengthen their market positions. They are widely believed directly to enhance corporate effectiveness and the ability to manage the turbulent waves of change. Creativity is now a core necessity for success in a profoundly changing world. Creativity is simply essential, because organizations and their environments are changing so dramatically. In the environment of change the intellectual capital held by companies is being recognized as the most important resource for sustaining competitive advantage. Creativity is recognized as the best way to leverage the intellectual capital that exists in every organization. The corporate culture must foster creativity and then turn it into the innovation that leads to competitive advantage.

The search for competitive advantage is enhanced through the following areas of corporate activity:

- *Continual change*: the effective management and implementation of change which can act as a catalyst for the creative process.

- *Continual innovation*: developing strategies for innovation and new product developments which increase investment in the leading-edge technologies. The focus on business development could also be used by the company to diversify its commercial options as a business.

- *Constant challenge*: developing a restlessness inside the company which challenges the expected mode of behaviour within the company. This restlessness would need to become part of the corporate culture. It would be necessary to challenge the expected behavioural norms in order to stimulate the company to adapt to the changing circumstances of the marketplace.

- *Renewing sources of competitive advantage*: the sources of advantage need to be upgraded, and the starting-point for many companies is to identify their distinct competencies and seek to build on their success. The availability of financial resources is crucial to enabling this process to take place.

- *Global sustainable approach*: the development of a *sustainable* competitive advantage is one of the most difficult tasks facing international managers.

The benefits of strategic management include the following:

- clear sense of vision;

- sharper focus on planning;

- sharper focus on implementation;

- understanding of the rapidly changing business environment.

A flexible approach to strategy formulation is now being encouraged by many practitioners, writers, commentators and academics. The idea that you can predict the future is now frowned upon, and there is a concerted effort to develop cohesive management teams which can design effective and flexible corporate strategies.

Strategy concerns the development of planning where any action can ensure the sustained long-term achievement of fast profitable growth and helps to eliminate cultural inertia, cultural inertia being anything which prevents the establishment of a lean and effective company. It concerns creative strategic planning and the way people inside and associated with the business *think*. Strategy is multidisciplinary and best operated at general management level, working closely with the board of directors. It is a long-term perspective on creativity not a short-term view.

Key components of a creative strategy

Future-oriented

The planning systems used in the company are firmly focused on the strategic development of the company and not the budget-setting exercise which takes place each year within many companies. Strategy formulation has to enable the company to boldly go to places which were unconceivable in the past.

Sharp objectives

The objectives which can be set by the creative company can be very specific and act as a motivatior to the creative teams within the organization. These objectives have to be realistic, challenging, measurable, timely and simple.

Effective coordination

The strategy designed by the company to assist creativity will have a positive effect on the coordination of activities in the organization. The strategy for creativity can help the organization finally to shed the skin of the old-style approach to innovation which is based on chaos or a single brilliant idea.

Setting standards of excellence

The strategy can establish standards of excellence throughout the creative teams in the company. This approach would take some of its lead from the total quality management concept but would be supported by the setting of *creative criteria* by the senior management team.

Re-energizing the process of strategy formulation

The ability to be creative will become a necessity in many organizations as they struggle to compete. A focus on creativity can work positively for any company because it can enable the management team to start by *re-educating* themselves in the creative skills needed for innovation to take place.

Tailored strategy models

The ideas and techniques that are used by organizations to develop their competitive strategies will vary. The key factor for many companies is the selection of systems which match the management style of the company. It is common to use external assistance from consultancy firms in the development of tailored approaches to strategic thinking but the external assistance acts only as a catalyst – the *real-time thinking* has to take place in the management team of the company.

Involving line management

The involvement of line management in the process of strategy formulation is a crucial factor in the success of the creative company. The line or function managers will be able to simplify the content of the strategy so that implementation of the strategy will actually take place. The *bottom-up* approach to strategic planning is imperative in developing a strategy for creativity. The lead needs to come from the senior management team but the problems of implementation have to be managed through a partnership between senior and line management.

Balanced source of ideas

The sources of ideas within your company will be varied but it is important to develop an *open management style* that can accept new strategic thinking to enable managers to feel confident in airing their views to the top team. The skills of senior management are important at this stage because a non-judgemental approach has to be adopted.

Targets for new product development

Target-seting is used consistently by creative companies and often has a real impact on the generation of new product ideas. It can focus the attention of line management on what needs to be achieved and can assist managers throughout the company in prioritizing and planning their activities.

Integrated by nature

To work effectively the strategic planning process has to be integrated into the operations of the business. It needs to be seen as a way of promoting entrepreneurial thinking and offering managers an opportunity to understand the future.

EXERCISE 2: Re-evaluating your corporate strategy

Conduct a short research project on your company to discover the approach the company has adopted towards strategy formulation for the medium- to long-term future of the business.

1   Outline the key elements of your company's corporate strategy:

2   What role does human resource management play in the development of your strategy?

3   Identify the areas of human resource expertise in your company:

4   Identify which actions need to be taken to implement an effective human resource management strategy:

5   How can these organizational changes be implemented in the short, medium and long term:

- comments:

- short term:

- medium term:

- long term:

EXERCISE REVIEW

You may find that your thinking focused on particular systems in the management of human resources or cultural or management style issues:

- the impact on the corporate culture of the business;

- increase in expenditure on the human resource strategy;

- change in the corporate structure of your business;

- the contrasting styles of your present company or companies you have experienced in the past.

Consider the exercise in relation to ideas already mentioned in this book.

Your personal objective: to ensure commitment to creativity

To ensure that creativity stays at the top of your organizational list of priorities you need to build commitment towards the concept and the practical realities of creativity. The innovation resulting from the creative process will not simply happen; it has to be fostered. This process has to be assisted by the strategist within the corridors of power in the company.

Seek creativity in every aspect of the company

The challenge is to seek innovation and creativity throughout the company. This means looking for creativity in *every* function of the business. The operational side of the business can be a source of creativity as well as the research and development (R&D) function and the marketing team.

Keep creativity at the centre of corporate thinking

It is important to re-engineer your corporate vision, mission and values to position creativity at the very heart of every business activity of the organization.

Introduce incentives to innovate

It is a good idea to introduce incentives to reward innovative ideas. Decide whether monetary rewards, recognition systems, annual ceremonies or badges of respect are most appropriate to your organization.

Foster involvement throughout the company

This involves increasing the freedom and empowerment of your people to enable them to work and think more creatively, and allow them to become fully involved in the decision-making process of the company.

Focus on management teamwork and cooperation

The acceptance of the team-based approach to creativity and the integrative *cross-fertilization of ideas* relies on the appointment of team leaders who enhance the creativity of your team yet do not stifle ideas or overshadow the contributions from team members.

Respect and promote individual contributions

Create the optimum-sized project groups to ensure *equality of contribution* from each individual by developing a hive of ideas and a series of new approaches to networking, and introduce the use of information networks and the development of cross-business cooperation within the company.

Focus on strategic leadership

Treat the concepts of strategy and leadership as separate yet interrelated and recognize that strategic leadership is essential to the success of your efforts to enhance the creativity of your business.

These changes and successes will not be achieved unless the senior management team has a focused and informed view of the importance of creativity and the need for a *strategic document* to support the process of innovation and creativity.

CHAPTER TWO

The creative corporate environment

This chapter will provide strategists with an understanding of some of the key components needed to develop a creative corporate environment within their companies. The right climate for dramatically improving creativity and innovation can be achieved by adapting your organization to a new and challenging business environment and by encouraging people to use their creative abilities and utilize the advantages of experimentation. You can raise the expectations regarding creative output by allowing for the possibility of discovering a totally new service, product or management system. To do this, place an emphasis on interdisciplinary teamwork and ensure that the corporate environment is a place of fun and a voyage of discovery for everyone involved in the creative process.

A series of *stepping stones* will be highlighted, which, if followed, will allow you to achieve the transformation required to shape the future of the company. This transformation is difficult to achieve and is often a gradual process which requires a focused and determined approach from the senior management team. Enhancing creativity in your company is one of the most difficult of management tasks because it involves motivating a large number of people with qualities normally associated with entrepreneurship, innovation and individual genius. These qualities include the following:

1 *Originality*: the ability to initiate new thinking is crucial to the success of the creative process. Original ideas will exist in your organization and can manifest themselves in positive or negative behaviour. It is the responsibility of the strategist to channel the behaviour of creative individuals towards creative activities. The starting-point is to create a corporate culture that does not suffocate originality but promotes *positive thinking*.

2   *Determination*: you should focus your intentions to foster the creative environment, and having a resolute purpose is necessary to steer the new environment towards success. Tenacity is important, to support the tough decisions and thinking which are often required for creativity to take place. It is also important to remove the blocks to the acceptance of innovation and creativity; these blocks may involve a lack of perceptual understanding of the creative concept, emotional reaction to changes in the corporate culture, new business methods, new business and working environment and the establishment of new parameters for thinking within the company.

3   *Continuous motivation*: senior management should be encouraged to *own* innovation and actively to promote it, communicating the importance of innovation by demonstrating the impact it has on the business. They must cultivate ideas and motivate people to achieve higher levels of success.

4   *Entrepreneurial flair*: entrepreneurial flair is difficult to recognize in some companies and may manifest itself in the following ways:

- having a desire to make things work more effectively;

- maintaining a feeling of excitement about your work;

- possessing the ability to share new business ideas;

- visualizing the stepping stones to help you achieve the introduction of a new business concept;

- managing difficult and stressful decisions;

- building networks for ideas to develop.

Supporting the proactive moves that are being made within the business and exploiting the changes in the business environment at every opportunity are positive signs of entrepreneurial flair. By developing a purposeful approach to entrepreneurship in the company you will encourage a predisposition towards risk-taking amongst the management teams. Do this by focusing on the introduction of innovative training and development strategies to support entrepreneurship throughout the company.

Many organizations will already exhibit pockets of individual genius, innovation and entrepreneurship. The line management of your company will be able to outline the examples of individual success (as in Exercise 3). It may be difficult for individual employees because the systems they are working with are designed to systemize activities rather than promote creative activities.

EXERCISE 3: The search for individual creativity

An interesting exercise would be to devise a questionnaire which focuses on the following key questions. The objective of the questionnaire would be to highlight the individual creative successes in your company. The questionnaire would be aimed at line managers and could be conducted on an interview basis.

1 How would you define creativity in your function/department?

2 What are the creative successes which have taken place in this function/department in the recent past?

3 Do you promote a culture of 'all ideas are welcome' in your function?

4 How can information technology be used to speed up the innovation process?

You can extend this series of questions to suit your particular company.

EXERCISE REVIEW

The exercise is aimed at identifying how line managers view creativity and innovation and the sources of both of these elements. It has the objective of identifying innovation and creative success in your company.

> Comments:

The challenge is to make creative actions a corporate way of life, rather than an occasional shock to the system and, consequently, to the individual involved; in other words, to make new thinking the norm and not the exception.

In a creative company the aim is to develop people who can work effectively in status-free teams, where the working environment promotes and protects individual ideas and facilitates the development of joint solutions. What imbues this process with meaning for people is not the fact of being part of a team but, rather, of sharing in creative achievements, the sense of pride and involvement at playing a role in designing or developing a new product, system or service and making it work. The starting-point is to establish a problem-solving and idea-generation culture which actually cuts across hierarchy and leads to action. A different set of decision-making channels and reporting lines will be needed. The creative company has constantly to re-examine work routines, explore different options and design new techniques. Companies will have to reaffirm their trust in people and encourage them to use neglected sources of creativity to build a solid foundation of new thinking within the company. If a company can be creative in everyday work practices, it can ensure that more levels of people within the company have the skills and opportunities to contribute to problem-solving, idea formulation and successful implementation of ideas.

Stepping stones to the creative company

The four steps to developing a creative company are outlined below and highlighted in Figure 2.1.

FIGURE 2.1   Stepping stones to the creative company

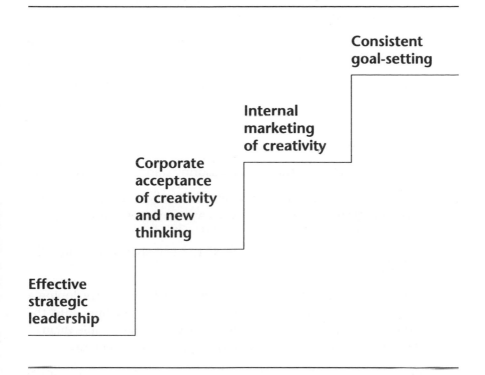

Step one: effective strategic leadership

Strategic leadership is fundamental to the success of the creative process in your company. It is crucial to have a board-level champion to provide the commitment, responsibility and impetus to promote and advance creativity. The appointment of a senior manager who believes in the key concepts of innovation and creativity is vital. The company should communicate the importance of innovation by consistently showing the impact it has on bottom-line performance, outlining and reinforcing the idea that creativity is part of the long-term strategy of the company and not a short-term panacea to the companies existing problems. The company must clarify the corporate interpretation of innovation and communicate these views to all the interested stakeholders.

The leadership role will be varied and will include the ability to sell the case and develop a role which includes the following aspects:

- leader as an innovator who shows the direction of the corporate efforts in creativity and innovation;

- leader as a visionary who can articulate the future impact of creative efforts in the company;

- leader as a symbol of the support for creative actions within the company;

- leader as a mobilizer who will motivate and focus other people's efforts in the right creative direction;

- leader as an auditor, setting and measuring standards of innovation;

- leader as an ambassador who represents the company at every opportunity and communicates the creative values of the company.

These actions will be translated through the key shapers of corporate actions in the company:

1 *Vision*: the focus of the vision statement will be on developing a clear view of the strategy needed to take the company into the future. The corporate vision has to excite people and enable them to own the concept of the future held by senior management.

2 *Mission*: the mission statement will concentrate on the operational aspects required to manage the business successfully and to motivate the employees within it.

3 *Business values*: the business values must contain creativity because the values of the company will help to shape the individual behaviours of people throughout the company. The business values will also assist managers in prioritizing the action plans they are developing on a continual basis.

CASE OUTLINE: ICL FUJITSU

Creativity has been recognized by ICL Fujitsu as a key factor in the future success of the business. The experience they have gained in operating in global markets has encouraged them to use strategic leadership as a weapon to achieve creativity. The company plan is to develop a creative corporate environment through the use of three key factors, which are outlined below.

The corporate mission statement

The mission statement is clear and aims to develop creative thinking within its people in order to build new business and long-term customer relationships. The value system of the company helps to support the redesign of business activities and the integration of information technology to support the creative process. The emphasis within the company has shifted towards a system in which products/services are developed with the customer and specifically tailored to the needs of their businesses.

The introduction of a new company culture

The company is attempting to promote creativity throughout the company and place the emphasis on an *integrated* form of work pattern. The introduction of self-directed learning has assisted this process and allowed individuals to explore the business development opportunities that emerge as part of their everyday work.

Successful management of change

The company has a strong attitude towards change which places a constant pressure on employees to adapt to change and manage the consequences. The acceptance of constant change is widespread throughout the company, and employees who do not experience some stages of change each year will be quite surprised. The management development strategy of the company is designed to strengthen the acceptance of change and to allow managers to deal with the pockets of resistance that may occur.

This is a long-term strategy and has been actively pursued over the last decade. This new approach has already produced a series of successes, including some recent creative initiatives. Business development consultants within one division offering professional/consulting services to existing and potential clients of the company identified service improvements through active teamwork and client contact. They were able to secure support from the senior management team in terms of advice and development finance. The origin of the new product came from a partnership developed with the client and based on consistent client contact. The product enabled the client to audit operations which had been difficult to manage in the past. The development of the new product was supported by the central training unit of the company through the use of self-managed learning. The product development process was also supported by a network of like-minded business developers who could exchange information and provide support on a regular basis. Problems have centred on the lack of management support and the lack of a clearly defined reward strategy.

The basic strategy of ICL Fujitsu is to combine the energy of individual employees and the creative process. The provision of skills is important and the company believes that it can reap the rewards of creativity by breaking down organizational barriers and reconstructing new networks of communication.[1]

Step two: corporate acceptance of creativity and new thinking

The corporate acceptance of creativity and new thinking is influenced by three key factors:

1   Intelligence and flexibility:

- available technology;

- available experience;

- potential technologies;

- assessment.

2   Corporate conditions:

- vision;

- strategy;

- structure;

- market insight;

- insight into business environment.

3   Operations:

- budgeting;

- planning and selection of projects;

- communications;

- performance indicators.

CASE OUTLINE: LEO BURNETT

Leo Burnett is promoting creativity and aiming to change employee mind sets from a *hierarchical* focus to a *creative* one. The environment has traditionally been dynamic and fast-moving but the competitive nature of the industry is placing the spotlight on corporate operations.

The company is under pressure to develop a more dynamic and creative environment. It has demonstrated to employees that the traditional culture governed by fear of failure and hierarchy is increasingly open to question. Emphasis is being placed on the skills of initiative and intuition to encourage individuals to be more creative. The company is training and developing employees not to accept the first and most obvious solution to a problem but instead to search for possible alternatives. Employees are encouraged not to reject any ideas which go against the normal behaviour of the creative team. The idea is to break down barriers by working with employees to reassure them that failure or poor ideas will not be viewed negatively but will be seen as part of the learning experience supported by senior management. The objective of the company is to encourage employees to be actively involved in multidisciplinary and diverse projects. These projects create a varied corporate experience and develop an open-minded approach to problem-solving.[2]

Step three: internal marketing of creativity

The principles of internal marketing can be applied to the introduction of a new corporate climate in your company. The company may experience difficulties in convincing the line managers in the company of the benefits of creativity and the positive impact it can have on the profitability of the business. The use of strategic information available to the strategic planner can have a major impact on the presentation of a lucid argument and the acceptance of strategic creativity in your company. The internal barriers to creativity can be immense and the challenge which confronts you should not be underestimated.

The strategic intent of your company may be out of line with the corporate capabilities of your business, or the aspirations of the senior management team may not be shared by the people who actually manage the operational side of the business. The resourcing of the internal marketing programme is crucial to its success, and the failure of senior management to recognize the importance of this issue is fatal to the prospects of creating the correct corporate environment. The implementation factors are too important to be left in the hands of the strategic planning function. If your company is seriously to improve the creativity that is taking place in the company a *transition management* group needs to be established to monitor and steer the process towards its successful completion.

Internal marketing can be used to develop an internal marketing framework to be utilized by the company to support the innovation management of your business. This framework will be based on generating support for the new climate of creativity through internal communication, incentives, leadership and coordination. Creative activities cannot be effectively implemented without the cooperation of the people who work within the company. The employees are the essential ingredient in the future success of your corporate climate and environment. They will have a direct impact on the success or failure of your creative initiatives because the promotion of creativity and the effective working of the process is very much linked to the actions of individuals in the company. Creativity is essentially based on the individual, which makes the marketing of the creative corporate environment to employees of your company all the more difficult.

The organization has to market its products and services externally and target a series of customer groups; a similar approach has to be adopted for the internal marketing of the concepts behind the creative process. It is imperative to work alongside the human resource management function; because of the nature of creativity you will need to examine the individual roles performed by employees and design attractive and creative roles for people which satisfy their individual needs. The managerial decisions taken by the company will involve the acceptance of new roles throughout the company. These decisions translate into a change of role and behaviour throughout the company from the chief executive officer, through the management teams, to the professional groups and business operations. The employees of the company will have to understand the thrust of the new creative orientation and the processes that underlie the concept.

The orientation towards creativity will be fostered by training and development on an individual level, but this will quickly expand to cover the offer of new skills and knowledge to teams and business units throughout the company. Training and development efforts will focus on skills but a continuous education programme will also be necessary to reinforce the concept of creativity and its importance in the future success of the business. This is one example of a programme which can be introduced to manage creativity more effectively; others will be explored later in this text.

A key factor in the success of these initiatives is the development of a *culture of cooperation* which assists the implementation of planning and the acceptance of the new working environment.

EXERCISE 4: Describing the creative corporate environment

Outline the indicators that give you confidence that an organization of your choice is aware of the importance of the factors we have discussed, including the focus on people, leadership, acceptance, objective-setting and internal marketing.

- Company (brief description):

- People factors:

- Leadership factors:

- Acceptance factors (resistance to change):

- Objective-setting factors:

- Internal marketing factors:

- Comments:

EXERCISE REVIEW

Once you have conducted this exercise you may find that the acceptance of change was quite high, but that the internal marketing of the new concepts was poorly managed and this had a direct impact on the performance of the company. Alternatively, you may find that the management of people was effective but the strategic vision of the organization was confusing, and that the lack of objective-setting could have been a factor in the failure of this particular corporate culture.

Step four: consistent goal-setting

The aim of the creative company is to set a series of goals for creativity and innovation which can act as a *pull-through mechanism* similar to that created by the pull of demand for products or services in some sectors of the economy. The setting of a series of goals can create a climate of productivity which continues to hit those goals set by senior management and leaves the organization asking for new achievement levels to be established. The aim is to manage the process successfully so that you can place a strong emphasis in your company on innovation and lead it towards creative success. The setting of new goals will help to create a corporate environment of continual improvement.

Successful creative companies establish a virtuous circle of creativity where innovation can take place and provide the company with the financial resources to reinvest in the creative process and maintain its competitive advantage. The role of goal-setting is to help managers throughout the company to accept the challenges facing them in the business environment and to provide them with the confidence to raise their game.

Successful companies like 3M would not state that their performance is based on the new invention or the brilliant idea, although the company has been world leader in many fields. It would support the notion that what makes the difference is deliberate and rigorous commitment to new product development within a corporate culture which is focused on the customer and which encourages individual creativity. The company believes that successful creativity requires a unique solution to customer needs and the ability to go beyond the customers' perceptions of their needs and to offer them new products which they may not previously have considered. The strategic leaders of the company see that creativity cannot be forced on people, but it can be encouraged. The encouragement of creativity is a key role for the senior management team and this encouragement can manifest itself in the development of the correct corporate conditions, where calculated risk-taking is accepted and actively supported.

The goal-setting that takes place in the company supports the development of this corporate culture. It enables managers to prioritize their actions and to design the operations of the business to meet the challenging goals that are set by the management team. The role of target-setting is not new and you can find examples of this approach in many forms in a host of companies, but it does seem to work in creative companies.

The senior management team will not be too concerned about setting the creative goals of the company, but will be more concerned about releasing the creative energies of the business to achieve those goals. The creative energies of the business can be released only in an environment which has developed a set of appropriate systems, procedures and processes to ensure the acceptance of the creative goals. The leadership and behaviour of senior management are important factors in the acceptance or otherwise of the creative process and the need for innovation in the company. The political pressures for non-acceptance will be strong, particularly if the results of creative efforts are not seen to bring immediate success. The whole concept may fall into disrepute if the strategic leadership is not fully behind the change in corporate environment. If the senior management team is not fully committed to the change and prefers a piecemeal approach, the political forces will be too strong and the undertaking will fail.

CASE OUTLINE: RANK XEROX

The approach used by Rank Xerox has some very good points. The company uses a system of objective-setting to manage the business. It may use this approach because of the historical background of the company, the nature of the industry or the desire for higher levels of cost-consciousness throughout the company. The objective-setting system has been adopted throughout the company and involves the establishment of clear objectives to be achieved by business areas within the company.

The objective for one business area could be to achieve higher levels of employee motivation and satisfaction, and the objective could be based on the previous goal set for the business area. The business area nominates an owner of the objective who manages and coordinates individual actions within the business area. A *measurement criterion* is established which can be based, as in this example, on employee satisfaction survey results. A series of actions are then agreed between the management team in the business area and individual reference details are given to the objective to monitor its progress. The measurement criterion is also applied to the individual actions taken by the management team and targets are set for each objective. There are problems in using this approach because many of the objectives facing the company will not revolve around creativity and the objectives designed to increase creativity may become lost in the general objectives of the company. This approach could be very effective in translating the broad corporate objectives into the business operations of your company.[3]

EXERCISE 5: Comparing aspects of the corporate environment

3M is a company which is often quoted as excellent in terms of innovation. The company suffers from the same problems as other companies who are attempting to innovate. The level of investment in research and development is high, with the company spending over $1 billion per year. The corporate goal of 30 per cent of their sales being due to come from products introduced in the last four years places pressure on the management team of the business, but this acts as a key driver for success. It is argued in 3M that this is the corporate goal that has the power to direct creative efforts within the company. The setting of goals is seen by 3M as an effective method of channelling effort and activity towards the ultimate corporate goal of customer satisfaction.

The company is consistent in its support for innovation and creativity, and recognizes that its innovation goals will not be a success on their own but that they have to be supported by consistent investment in new and emerging technologies.

■ How does the approach of your company compare with that of either 3M or a close competitor in your market?

■ Examine this chapter and make a list of the important factors that you believe contribute to the success of a creative corporate environment.

■ When you have constructed your list of key factors compare those factors to what seems to happen in your competitor's company or 3M and contrast this information with your own organization.

■ Do the stepping stones outlined in this chapter appear in your organization?

	3M/Competing company	Your company
1		
2		
3		
4		
5		
6		
7		
8		
9		
10		

- Comments:

EXERCISE REVIEW

You may be surprised by the similarities between your organization and 3M. The differences may centre on the level of investment in the process of innovation or research and development. The focus on 3M may give you a starting-point to think about the key issues and to design a relevent strategic document or convene a management workshop to discuss the points raised by your analysis.

The foundations of business transformation

The successful strategist will work with senior management in achieving a gradual transformation in the organizational culture. The starting-point for many strategists will be understanding the business environment and the benefits of enhancing the corporate environment to encourage creativity.

The strategic stepping stones outlined above and in Figure 2.1 will form the foundations of the transformation that will take place in your organization. These stepping stones need to be supported by a series of corporate initiatives which will transform strategy into action.

Promoting a problem-solving and idea-generation culture

This can include the introduction of idea-generation systems into the organization or, alternatively, the review and modernization of existing systems. Alongside these systems could be a series of recognition awards for creative ideas or projects successfully introduced into the organization. The introduction of idea-generation systems would require a development plan aimed at providing people in the organization with the problem-solving capability needed to make these systems work effectively.

Matching the changing needs of customers and the business environment

An awareness of the changing needs of the customer and the overall business environment is required to ensure that the initiatives being taken are appropriate and build a successful partnership with the customer. A close working partnership must develop between the corporate planning and human resource management functions of the organization. The maxim of being close to the customer has to be tested to decide whether the creative initiatives being tried by the organization are indeed delivering enhanced customer benefits.

Relearning how to trust employees

The organization may believe that trust exists between the employees of the organization and the senior management team. This can be tested by using employee attitude surveys or internal feedback sessions. The areas that need to be explored include the percentage of ideas being generated internally, customer ideas or external research and development, and the number of new internal ideas that are being implemented. In addition, the reward and recognition system can start to be explored to see how closely it matches individual and team effort within the company.

Introducing comprehensive communication systems

A comprehensive communication system needs to be in place to publicize the existence of the idea-generation systems and the reward and recognition procedures and to reinforce senior management commitment towards the creative environment. The concept of creativity needs to be promoted flexibly and effectively. Senior management will have to evidence their commitment to the creative environment through their actions.

The communications system is one method that can be used by the organization to encourage creativity but it needs to be supported by the innovation targets set by the company. The mission statement can refer to the need for creativity or innovation in the organization and can give employees the green light to take action. New product development targets can be set by senior management in negotiation with individual business units; these can act as a guide to success for every individual within the business. The company values may already include a reference to creativity or innovation, but a reinterpretation may prove worthwhile for any company as a method of refocusing employees' efforts.

Training and development strategies to support creativity

The role of the training and development strategy will provide support for people attempting to enhance their creative input. The use of discussion groups is a good starting-point in understanding the training and development needs of the company. The training opportunities need to be publicized by the company in order to entice line management and individuals to explore the advantages of training and development.

Business development through people

The communications programme should raise the level of interest in creativity across the company. Once the interest is established the company will need to satisfy the desire within people to take action. This action has to be coordinated at line-management level and any actions taken need to be directed at the customer in the form of business development. This approach can be used by private- and public-sector organizations. Individuals are given the responsibility to design and implement business or project ideas through their close working relationship with the customer.

Investment in creative people, products and organization

Investment in any organization is governed by myriad pressures and the support for creative activities in the company is going to have to compete with other areas of demand within the business. The initial challenge is to recognize the importance of the creative process and, once investment has been agreed, to ensure that the investment is consistently available to enhance the creative response of your company.

The *creative behaviour* of the people in the organization is a key factor to consider when the implementation of a creative corporate environment is being considered. Training seminars can be arranged on a regular basis which support the creative activities taking place in the company. These seminars would aim to deliver a positive message to employees concerning the expected behaviour and actual behaviour of employees involved in the creative process. The key aim is to give new ideas an opportunity to develop and grow in a positive environment, as transformation starts with people exhibiting positive behaviour.

The corporate *targets* for new product development will already have been set by senior management, but to complement these targets individual objectives have to be set by the line managers involved in the creative process. The process of setting objectives has to be clear, but more importantly the human resource function has to monitor the level of confidence in the present system and attempt to provide methods that could assist managers to develop the level of confidence required for effectiveness. This objective-setting could take the form of departmental and functional objectives which take their lead from the corporate objectives.

The human resource management effort in this instance will focus on the need to manage the development needs of people involved in the creative process and to investigate the development requirements of functional groups and how they integrate with other departments. The work of the creative people within organizations is based on the concept of interdisciplinary cooperation, and the future requirements of this approach need to be carefully assessed and developed.

This initiative would support the efforts being made in the design of organizational development initiatives but the emphasis here is fundamentally on *enabling* your organization to behave like a small company though the company may be a large international multinational. This involves engendering in the organization the ability to listen to small ideas as well as the new breakthroughs that have an obvious application in the marketplace, and developing a culture where anyone can speak to the top management team of the organization on an informal basis without feeling that it is a privilege. This promotes a culture of informality and cooperation and reinforces the open-door policy of the creative company.

The financial incentives that are provided for company personnel need to be aimed at three levels: individual, team and corporate. The financial incentives have to be linked to the implementation of the corporate environment as well as the achievement of corporate goals relating to success in creativity.

EXERCISE 6: Determining aspects of the corporate environment

Let's consider your own company and perhaps the key questions that you need to ask relating to how your company utilizes people effectively in its drive to achieve strategic creativity.

1   What are the key elements of your company's creative advantage?

2   What role do people play in the development of this advantage?

3   What are the areas of human resource expertise in your company?

4   Which initiatives need to be taken to implement an effective corporate environment that enhances creativity?

5   How can these corporate changes be implemented in the short, medium and long term?

- Comments:

- Short term:

- Medium term:

- Long term:

EXERCISE REVIEW

You may find that your thinking focused on particular systems used in the management of human resources in your company, including:

- development policies;

- career structures;

- incentives and recognition;

- corporate structure;

- training and development;

- confusion over the role of the human resource strategist.

These are some of the organizational changes that could be initiated by the strategist. These changes can start the process of transformation that will inevitably lead to an enhancement of the corporate environment and the achievement of strategic change.

CHAPTER THREE

Innovation and the opportunities for the strategic planner

This chapter will look at the key components of the innovation management process and examine the opportunities available to the strategic planning function to assist their organizations in achieving success in this activity. Creativity is found in the processes that develop new products and also in the methods used to design new services. The opportunities for the strategic planning manager lie in considering the strategic and structural changes that may be needed in the company to assist in the implementation of the new processes. The effective strategist will need to examine the business environment in detail and position the company successfully in the 'new reality'. Changes may be required in a variety of key areas of activity within the company, for example new skill sets for people, new methods or techniques for generating new ideas, and new corporate structures and systems to facilitate the introduction of new products and services into the marketplace.

The very nature of innovation provides the strategic planning specialist with an opportunity to intervene in the process and have a direct impact on its success or failure. The innovation process is dependent on a series of people communicating across an often complex organizational structure, liaising on a regular basis and promoting cooperation in the pursuit of success. People are continually *networking* and interacting in different ways that help to cut across functions and encourage new thinking within the company. Motivation is needed to maintain momentum and to implement a strategy for improved innovation. Consider the following examples:

■ A global medical company has one executive whose sole responsibility is to work with the individual subsidiaries of the company and coordinate company thinking on new product and service ideas and to allocate resources for new product development.

- A Canadian-based financial consultancy employs one manager with no job description but a very broad remit to initiate and coordinate new thinking in order to facilitate new business development.

- A leading British international company uses the headquarters strategic planning function to motivate country managers throughout the world to generate and develop new ideas and opportunities for overseas expansion.

The innovation process in any company is designed around the effective general management of people and their *inherent creativity*. The role of the strategic planning manager can be very important if her or his interventions or ideas are seen to have a direct impact on the success of innovation. The role of the strategic planning manager is to advise on the construction and implementation of new systems that can smooth the design of the product or service and its delivery to the customer.

The standard approach used by companies to generate new products or services will follow many of the stages outlined in Figure 3.1. The idea-generation stage is crucial to the success of new product/service development and this will involve a series of techniques designed to highlight the opportunities available to your company. Creativity is viewed as essentially an individual activity, but many companies will use a team-based approach in their search for new ideas and business opportunities. The marketing function plays an important role in generating ideas, but many strategists are now recognizing that there is often a pool of human resources in the company who are not given the opportunity to voice their ideas.

You need to assess which techniques for idea-generation will work most effectively in your company. Encourage individuals to use the right- and left-hand sides of their brains. Explore the differences between individual, small-group and corporate idea-generation. The key focus has to be on enabling people in your company to use their imagination in examining the business development opportunities open to them.

The theory is that each stage can be successfully managed in close succession. This approach would seem to present very few problems for companies, but, as experience has proved, many companies find that the pressures on new product development for immediate and sustained success place unbearable strains on the process. The idea-generation techniques used by companies need to be appropriate to the effective management of the company, and the screening of original ideas has to be comprehensive yet fair and not stifle the creative process. Concept development and testing may appear to be a relatively straightforward

FIGURE 3.1   Standard approach to generating new products/services

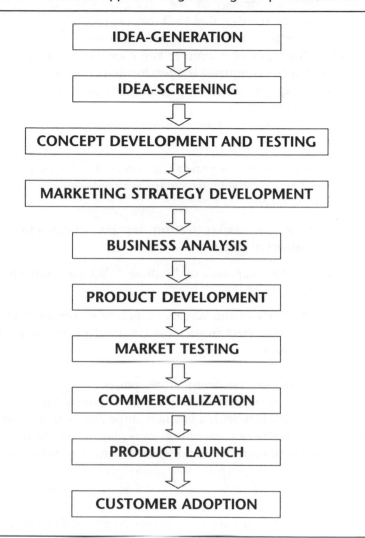

process but there is a strong need for constant testing of the initial concept as the marketplace is often very dynamic. It is difficult to monitor this situation and to prevent it from developing into chaos.

The strategy formulated around the new product/service needs to be carefully considered and to complement the new product/service development process, not hinder it. One question which is at the forefront of senior managers' thinking is when is the best time to commence work on the formulation of a *new innovation strategy*. Some companies may choose to develop the new strategy at the idea-generation stage and other companies may take the view that the creative process needs to be free of any restrictions before the final strategy is fully considered.

Product development is another key issue to consider because the pressure within many companies is often focused on shortening the cycle of development against preset management targets, in order to drive down development costs.

Market testing also has a series of major considerations, which may include:

- the detail and extent of testing that needs to take place to provide marketing and general management with a degree of confidence in its eventual success;

- a review of the market testing process which supports the commercialization stage;

- an analysis of the approach to the product launch and the prospects of the new product;

- a detailed review of the success or failure of the product/service launch and the direct impact on the level of adoption by your customer groups.

Products and services are becoming more complex to design and build as organizations fight to differentiate their products and services from those of their competitors. It is often a business imperative that this process is speeded up, and strategic planning can play a significant role in supporting and developing the innovation strategies of your company.

EXERCISE 7: Does your approach to innovation provide you with competitive advantage?

Effective innovation processes are difficult to construct and implement in a dynamic business environment. The key driving force behind many of the changes affecting innovation processes has been the unpredictable nature of the competitive threat. In response to new pressures in the competitive environment, managers find it difficult to develop a system which can adequately deal with the external threat. Competitive information enables you to understand the response of the competition prior to them taking action to improve systems.

Consider a series of improvements which could be made in the following components of your innovation process to provide you with competitive advantage and outline your views below.

- increasing the speed to market of new products and services:

- streamlining your corporate innovation process:

- improving the control of the innovation process:

- ensuring that the process of innovation is linked to an effective business plan:

- implementing an effective planning process to support the innovation process:

Examine each aspect of the new product/service development process to identify improvements or changes that you believe can have a significant impact on the innovation process.

- idea-generation:

- idea-screening:

- testing and marketing strategy:

- business analysis:

- development:

- commercialization:

- product/service adoption:

EXERCISE REVIEW

You may find that this exercise leaves some major gaps in the understanding of your corporate innovation process. Spend one hour, preferably with colleagues, constructing an action plan which can concentrate on the problems experienced in the development of an improved system of innovation.

Strategies for innovation in leading companies

Innovation strategies are being revised by companies on a regular basis and these reviews normally involve the matching of technology, resources and people in a search for competitive advantage. The introduction of new techniques for innovation is a difficult task and needs to be considered very carefully by senior management. The selection of people for new product development teams, the structure of the organization, the motivation of individuals and the formation of effective teams are key issues for the business development and product development managers of creative companies.[1]

The interventions that can be made by the strategic planning function will involve consultancy advice to key managers involved in the business development process and managing resources to assist managers in achieving greater success in the development of new products/services. The strategist will need to establish criteria for allowing new ideas to flow through the innovation process. The aim is to allocate resources effectively so that winners can be identified and given the green light to proceed. 'Gates' can be used to force go/no-go decisions and enable the quick kill at any stage of your development process.

The use of portfolio analysis across the new product development process can be an effective method of speeding up the production of common functional elements and managing technological platform developments. The return on investment of new product development activities can be highlighted to encourage improvements in the innovation process. Using early market testing procedures allows strategy to emerge in a creative manner. You can achieve continuous improvement by using the process data base to re-weight criteria and increase the speed and productivity of activities over a predetermined timescale.

You will need to work alongside managers to help maintain a momentum for the innovation process and the development of the members of product development teams. It is also important to appoint a team leader who will enhance the creativity of your team yet not stifle ideas or overshadow the contributions of every team member. Try to promote cross-divisional cooperation to achieve shared ownership of the innovation and prevent internal disputes over idea ownership. The objective is to funnel individual ideas to the rest of the group so that they can be developed and enhanced.

The design of the new product development systems used by companies can be assisted by actively involving the customer in the development stages and increasing the use of two-way communication and the development of an in-depth understanding of customer trends. Invite the most appropriate customers to be involved in the concept development and idea-screening stages, and then use multidisciplinary teams to turn ideas, data, attitudes and comments into viable commercial information to form the basis of product/service development.

You should identify the people-management issues at the outset of new business development projects, rather than bolting on the development needs as the project develops, and work alongside the internal/external organizational development specialists to maximize the performance of the new product development team from the outset of the new project. The identification of individual, task and group needs is important, with the development of strategy and development workshops to match.

The processes used to motivate are important to ensure that enthusiasm and action are consistent factors in the successful management of the innovation process. They help team members to enjoy a higher level of ambiguity and flexibility and to maintain strong levels of motivation despite these difficulties.

Development methods can be extensive and may include the following:

- group-focused workshops which can clearly define team objectives and new product/service specifications;

- training seminars which can focus on specific team needs;

- individual development contracts which will reinforce individual development needs and not allow them to be overshadowed by the needs of the team.

- creativity skills enhancements aimed at maintaining the driving force of new ideas into the team/innovation/creative process.

Selection systems should be based on the need for creative people who can generate ideas and maximize their creative contribution to the overall success of the company. They should place a greater emphasis on the skills of initiative and introduce intuition to encourage individuals to be more creative.

Institute reward strategies for creative ideas and decide what are the best forms of reward for your company. These could take the form of monetary rewards based on performance, recognition systems focusing on individual or group achievements, awards concentrating on business unit successes or ceremonies highlighting group successes.

The strategic planner needs to be involved in the design and development of the innovation process if her or his full contribution is to be recognized by line management. The product managers will realize that her or his door is open and that s/he can make a legitimate contribution to the design as well as the management of the innovation process.

The design of the innovation processes within companies will have some basic similarities, in that it will in every case require a process from idea-generation through to commercialization, as highlighted in Figure 3.1.

The difficulty arises when matching working methods used by the company to the design of the system. The key challenge is to be able to take a strategic and objective view of your company rather than viewing your company with its old and well-established customs and practices. It is important to view the company as a *greenfield site opportunity*, i.e. as a new entity. This task is difficult to achieve but can be organized and managed by using a multidisciplinary and diverse team to see the company as if through a new pair of eyes.

A series of case outlines can be discussed which show a variety of methods used to assist in the design of their new innovation systems. The system used by 3M is driven by a high level of investment in technology; the central focus of innovation at Rank Xerox is the use and management of the creative team; the key aspect of the system at Motorola is to match the requirements of the market to business development; and the fundamental issue in service design in the health sector is the management of resources and their effect on the creative process. In the rest of this chapter I have highlighted these central themes and how they apply to each company example.

EXERCISE 8: Opportunities open to the general manager

Choose two business units/divisions of your company to examine in some detail.

- Brief description of the present system:

- Business unit/division 1:

- Business unit/division 2:

Once you have chosen the business unit/division, suggest a series of methods that are used to manage innovation within those particular business units/divisions.

	Method	Business unit/division 1	Business unit/division 2
1			
2			
3			

4

5

6

Compare the methods used by both of the business units/divisions on a scoring system based on 100 per cent. The objective is to assess whether they have improved the effectiveness of your business operations; if not, why not?

EXERCISE REVIEW

This exercise should enable you to outline the innovative systems used by your organization and to compare the effectiveness of those systems in the two business units/divisions of your choice.

It is imperative continuously to review your innovation systems, structure and creative people, as this aspect of the business is finally being recognized as a source of competitive advantage. The companies that have successfully converted their innovation strategies into new products/services have taken market leadership in their chosen sector. Companies will have to create the correct corporate structure to suit the needs of the individual rather than the needs of the company. The focus will be placed on the individual motivation of creative employees in an interdependent network of innovative success.

CASE OUTLINE: 3M

The innovation process at 3M centres on the ability to support a high level of investment in new technology and to match this with an innovative corporate culture. The new product development systems used by the company allow flexibility in the generation of new ideas and the transformation of those ideas into tangible products and services. There are lessons to be learned from this approach which can be used by any organization and can form the basis of a new approach to the support given to the process of creativity.

The corporate goals and vision statements of senior management within 3M lay the foundations for new business, service and product development activity within the company. The success of innovation rests on a high level of investment in new technology. These technologies are divided into two groups:

1 The technology platform group.

2 The embryonic and developing technologies.

These technologies act as a driver for the innovations conceived and developed by the company, and the technology platform group acts as a basis for new products presently in the market. They may produce the following types of products:

- adhesives;

- films;

- optics;

- imaging;

- drug delivery.

Examples of embryonic and developing technologies, which form the next phase of innovation, may include:

- flat-panel displays;

- diamond-like films;

- filtration;

- mechanical fasteners.

The investment in the basic technologies acts as a strategic driver for building the entrepreneurial culture of the company. The technologies are constantly challenged, improved or replaced by the company and they act as a springboard for innovative activities within the company. New products are viewed by managers, professionals and technologists as being the main source of customer satisfaction and customer retention. The company has the ability to identify and exploit new technologies very successfully and to put in place systems that maximize the company benefits derived from the variants of these technologies. 3M supports the investment in technology by establishing a clear set of company values that can be utilized by everyone within the company. This approach assists employees, and particularly managers, when a decision is to be made regarding a new product or service concept. It alleviates the difficulty often experienced by managers when making decisions which may have an uncertain outcome.

There is a clear focus on the ability of the company to measure what is important and to identify activities that strongly support the achievement of success:

- Positive competition is encouraged with the objective of developing a set of competencies in innovation.

- New product development objectives are continually revised.

- The creation of an almost *tribal culture* which focuses managers' attention on the need to create and develop new opportunities for the company.

- Development activities are concentrated on products and services that are new to the market and contain features that are not available to existing customers.

- The thinking of technologists is focused on the adaptation of existing products and services and not necessarily on the development of brand new product or service concepts.

The ultimate aim of the innovation process at 3M is based on listening to customers, identifying their changing needs and future challenges. This is underpinned by the ability of all levels of employees to be self-critical and to focus on individual, group and corporate achievement.

CASE OUTLINE: RANK XEROX

The central focus of innovation in Rank Xerox is the creative team. The team is usually set up to manage and launch the new product and is involved in the total process from idea-generation through to product launch. This product or service may emerge from the research and development centres in Palo Alto, California, Grenoble or Cambridge.

The Business Development Team will comprise the following members, who will be chosen on the basis of their track record in innovation:

- director of design and development;

- design and development team;

- logistics;

- finance;

- personnel officer;

- product launch team;

- manufacturing;

- marketing.

This structure was established following a business process re-engineering project which took place in the early 1990s. The unit is responsible for direct profits from the new product/service. The benefit of this approach is that information and decision-making can be effectively coordinated. A weakness in this approach is that the team can become too task-specific and avoid the strategic issues of the new venture which may be related to increased performance.

Strategic guidance from within the company is vitally important to ensure the success of the Business Development Team. This guidance will include two key elements:

- competitive scanning;

- appropriate customer and product match.

Focus groups are established on a frequent basis to test the acceptance of a product or service. They are supported by independent market research and consist of customers, sales and service people. A series of observers are used by the company to comment on the development process and they work in close collaboration with the marketing team. Intensive activity takes place to establish and launch a new product into the market. The process of business development is very carefully considered and implemented within the company (see Table 3.1). Market testing

TABLE 3.1   The idea-generation and product development process

1 Marketing definition review	First cut of the business case
	Revenue expected
	Development costs
	Return on investment
	Profit before tax
	Resources required
	People required
2 Preconcept phase	Review
	Engineering response
	Probability of producing the product/ service
3 Concept phase	The initial concept will be finalized
4 Review	Prior to issuing drawings and tooling resources
5 Design	Financial resources will be considered in some detail
6 Product	Resources to be introduced into the innovation process
7 Field testing	Internal and external
8 Final production machinery	
9 Product launch	

would take place in the UK and the USA and would draw on specific criteria appropriate to the launch of the product or service.

The development of a totally new product may take up to two years and a variant of an existing product may take up to six months. Prior to the marketing definition review the electrical, mechanical and production functions will make an unofficial choice of resources. This will be supported by weekly team meetings until the end of the preconcept stage. The technical programme manager is usually coordinating these activities within the company, and fifty to 100 people may be involved in the whole process at any one time.

The innovation process used by the company is very well developed and has a strategic position in the working methods of the company, and it forms a key focal point for the activities of the creative teams of the company. It is crucial to ensure that the system is responding to the needs of the market and also the needs of people in the company. The system may be very well established in the company but the interaction between the needs of the company and the individual has constantly to be explored.

CASE OUTLINE: MOTOROLA

The basic aim of the innovation process within Motorola is to match the correct products/services to market requirements. The approach is dynamic, the dynamism stemming from the needs of the market, which are becoming increasingly pressurized and variable. The company can set up a Business Development Team at short notice to drive forward the innovation process. This team acts as a catalyst for the development of new products in any of the groups within the company. The group is composed of the following people:

- business development manager;

- business development director;

- product manager.

The new business development process is driven by the need to penetrate markets by using new products and to generate an increasing number of potential new businesses through those products. The combination of a strategic business plan, marketing effort and management development programme can make the difference between success and failure in the innovation process.

These teams are made up of a combination of specialists from different fields, including technical and mechanical design, distribution, finance, manufacturing, software engineering and test and operations. The key aims of these teams are to engender a sense of ownership of new concepts and to shorten the time to market from idea-generation to product launch. The role of the product manager is crucial and requires a set of skills which are difficult to find in one individual:

- a clear technical awareness;

- general management expertise;

- marketing and sales skills;

- market understanding;

- negotiating ability;

- interpersonal skills of the highest order;

- an awareness of group dynamics.

The products launched in Europe are often variants of existing products, which create their own set of problems and management issues. The tailoring of US products to the European market has become a major concern of the innovation teams in the UK.

The driving force of the innovation process within Motorola is focused on the need for a very clear understanding of the requirements of the market and an effective development team. The strategic planning interventions are people-centred, and a great deal of benefit can be derived from a sense of strategic leadership and from an innovation strategy being in place.[2]

CASE OUTLINE: HEALTH SECTOR

Financial support for the innovation process is crucial to its success, in terms not only of overall financial support for the new product or service, but also of the financial support for the recruitment and selection, training and development, motivation, and reward and recognition of individuals involved in the process. The investment in the innovation process has to be consistent and secure if the new project is to gain any real credibility and to survive the often competitive environment of organizations where managers may be competing fiercely for limited resources.

The financial resources that are made available on a national level have to be supported at a local level in order for a new project to be successful. For example, the King's Fund Centre for Health Services Development manages a scheme, the logical underpinning of which is based on the promotion of new practice development within particular sections of the service, particularly nursing. The practice development has to be clearly a new concept or idea in nursing to gain financial support from the King's Fund Centre, i.e. differentiated. The key to differentiating each new idea on service provision is to develop a coherent strategy for the development of a service and to ensure that the new idea is contributing to the new culture within the health sector. The financial support which is offerred by the King's Fund is really pump-priming finance to enable new projects to commence and to enter a period of stability, and consequently growth.

The financial support once the project has commenced is provided by local management, where the new venture or idea has been introduced. This process is quite effective at launching new ideas and concepts but relies on the support of local management to ensure the success of the project.

The role of the strategist in this instance is to act as a focal point for the development team in securing more financial resources for the people needed on the project or for new expenditure. The effective strategic planner needs to be aware of the factors that impact on the success of the innovation process, in order to design systems and processes that assist business development and reinforce the need for successful implementation.[3]

Factors in successful innovation

The factors impacting on successful innovation can be placed into three stages.

Stage 1

- Constant support from senior management.

- Strategic leadership.

These are fundamental to the success of your innovation process.

Stage 2

- Consistent financial support.

- Achievement monitoring.

The financial support for some creative initiatives in companies may decline as the project becomes live. This must not be allowed to happen. Setting and monitoring achievements and targets is essential to the success of the innovation process in your company.

Stage 3

- Selection of creative people.

- Team-based problem-solving techniques.

- Motivation of creative people.

- Developing new challenges to maintain quality.

The selection of creative people can help to maintain the drive within the project team. The momentum of enthusiasm towards the project has to be maintained at a high level. Team-based problem-solving techniques such as multidisciplinary *tiger teams* are used by the company to break the usual rules in order to reduce product development time.

EXERCISE 9: Opportunities open to the strategic planner

Review the main activities that occupy your time and compare your activities with the internal/external activities listed below.

Your activities:

Internal challenges	*External challenges*
corporate culture	market shifts
management skills	competition
management commitment	economic restructuring
financial challenges	political change
innovation	technological change
operational problems	social/environmental factors
strategic planning process	

EXERCISE REVIEW

You may find that your activities are more focused on the internal issues of corporate culture, management skills, management commitment and innovation than you first thought. These areas are important activities to be considered when improvements in the process of innovation are taking place.

CHAPTER FOUR

Selection of creative people

The people that drive the creative process in your organization are your creative assets and their effective selection is paramount to the overall success of creativity and innovation in your organization. Microsoft became a world leader in computer software production through effort, astute technological and business acumen, and careful management of the corporate culture. The corporate culture is based on empowerment, and power is delegated to the software developers who write and design the software. The company is managed in such a way that managers interact as little as possible with the developers, although management does provide mentors to help newly recruited software developers to understand and work within the corporate culture. Selection is the starting-point for the creative process and it is important that strategic planning and human resource strategists formulate a relevant selection strategy for the company.

Creative people of the future will demand more from your company. They will demand that you provide them with significant opportunities for development and to use their creative skills. The concept behind a career structure is changing, and creative people are recognizing that their competitive advantages are based on the marketability of their personal skills and not the fact that they have been employed for a number of years by a company. The selection of creative people will have to reflect these changes and companies will be adopting selection strategies which identify a new set of competencies based on cultural fit and opportunities to use the latent skills of each individual to the maximum. The needs of the company and the individual will have to match if real creative success is to become a reality.

This chapter will focus on the selection systems used by leading companies and explain why the selection process is such a fundamental prerequisite for success in a creative company. The creativity of any organization is based on the everyday actions of the people it employs. Leading companies have clearly identified the link between corporate strategy and objectives and the correct selection of the right people to ensure that they are achieved. The matching of the corporate strategy and the selection process is very important and needs to be an integral part of the people-management strategy of the company. This calls for a very high level of awareness within the human resource management function of the corporate strategy of the company and its likely effects on the human resource requirements of the future.

In the example of MicroSoft, the role of the senior management team is to create the right corporate culture which can allow people to have their own independent beliefs yet focus on the fact that interdependence is essential to the success of any of their endeavours. This point must be recognized by the strategists in the human resource function and strategic planning as they construct selection systems for the future.

Selecting creative people is a difficult task because there are so many intangibles and unpredictable factors to consider. The type of company obviously has an influence on the individuals attracted to apply in the first place. The applicants for a role in a leading advertising agency in central London with offices throughout the world will have different aspirations and perceptions from a new recruit to a pioneering team breaking new ground in the world of medicine.

Medical aspirations	*Advertising aspirations*
breakthrough focus	financial rewards
community spirit	travel
professionalism	creative independence
confidentiality	individual exposure
access to support	access to expertise

Creativity in the health sector may require individuals who are motivated by the chance of professional enhancement and security of employment rather than the pure financial rewards that exist in the financial sector. The motivations of a trader earning £100,000+ per year will be very different from those of a young medical professional who may have a very similar educational and social background.

In creating selection systems, the aspects to focus on will include:

- the corporate philosophies which support the methods of selection being used by leading companies;

- the individual attributes needed to ensure sure that creative people take up the challenge of building a creative company;

- the concepts used by leading companies and the criteria on which selection can be based;

- the possible systems available to a creative company;

- the attributes to search for in prospective employees.

The selection systems used by creative companies are not necessarily very different from those of other companies but they place a strong emphasis on the desires and needs of the individual employee and not just the needs of the company (see Figure 4.1).

FIGURE 4.1 Comparison of corporate and people needs

CORPORATE NEEDS ⟹ SIMILARITIES ⟸ PEOPLE NEEDS

Clear responsibilities

Commitment

Positive reward systems

Opportunities for challenge

Opportunities for expression

Opportunities for development

Reasons for decisions

Information

Higher understanding of business

Increased involvement

Teamwork and individual growth

Strategic leadership

Management competency

Consistency of work

EXERCISE 10: Compare and contrast corporate and individual needs in your company

Using Figure 4.1 as a basis for your thinking, prepare a list of factors which you believe to be important to your company in its search for a competitive advantage through creativity.

	Your company needs	*Individual needs*
1		
2		
3		
4		
5		
6		
7		
8		
9		
10		

Spend twenty minutes considering the similarities between these lists and review the strategic or operational initiatives which could be undertaken by your organization to improve the overall effectiveness of people management.

- Comments:

EXERCISE REVIEW

The needs of your company and those of individuals may seem to be at odds, but as you examine them in some detail you may discover many similarities. Issues to consider include:

- The practical implementation of new people strategies:

- The reasons why you cannot introduce any of these initiatives:

■   The corporate benefits that may be derived from the introduction of new initiatives:

Creative companies have to give people time to express their ideas and views on how they would like to contribute to the success of your company. Senior management will involve each individual in developing a set of creative achievements which will form the basis of the selection process. Individuals will be asked to generate new creative ideas for how they can contribute to the future corporate creativity of the company. Once the parameters of creative activity have been agreed the company can explain to prospective employees how their creativity will be enhanced throughout their time with the company. This agreement will form the basis of a development, which will be monitored and managed not only by the company but also by the individual.

There are some key differences in the selection process used by the creative organization:

■   an emphasis on the role of the company as a facilitator and not a director of the behaviour of each individual;

■   the provision of opportunities for individuals to develop their own creative skills;

■   a strong bias towards a joint approach which is influenced by the needs of the market and the individual.

The internal sources of creative people will be important, and consistent monitoring of the creative performance of individuals and the provision of training and development support are crucial. An awareness of the needs of managers has to be gained by the strategic planning professionals, in order to make a valid contribution to the selection process.

The human resource management function will need to understand the new technologies being developed by the company and their impact on future product/service development projects within the company. The function will start to behave in a similar fashion to an internal agency searching for new talent to be used on projects, rather than administering selection procedures. The function will also have to understand the detail of the competitive analysis being conducted by the strategic planning professionals to compare corporate needs and people requirements for the future.

Competition for that rare commodity of creativity in people will be fierce. The pressures generated by the business environment will intensify. Future success will be based on the speed and effectiveness with which companies enable their people to transform ideas and new concepts into products, services and new management systems. Companies can derive a competitive advantage from continuous and dynamic creativity and the refinement of a variety of ideas that may come from any part of the organization. The key message is that creativity will not be the sole prerogative of senior management or the business founders; it will be a capability and behavioural change that will be diffused throughout the company.

CASE OUTLINE: ICL FUJITSU

This company has a selection system that recognizes that creativity is not the sole prerogative of senior management. ICL Fujitsu focuses on the ability of potential employees to look at markets through new eyes. The company is forecasting that its marketplace will become very fragmented and that it requires a different approach towards business development than that previously considered.

The skills of the customer-facing people in the company have to equip each person with the ability to spot and develop business opportunites. The introduction of new ways of working to support these skills is enabling the company to seize profitable market segments by presenting products and services to customers in new ways. These new approaches are managed and led by creative people who have a flexible view of the market they are operating in and understand very clearly the needs of the individual customer.

The company thinking behind the selection process is that the future success of the company will hinge on carefully listening to customers and designing products and services around their views. The difficulty faced by the company is in supporting this basic philosophy and managing the processes that enable people to be creative in finding solutions in response to customers' views and feedback.

Creative people are vital to ICL Fujitsu and the role of the strategist has become central in establishing a strong link between the marketing function of the business, human resource management and strategic planning. The role of the strategist in ICL Fujitsu is to ensure that once creative people are in place, they are given decision-making responsibility and are trusted to build long-term relationships with the customer.

The management skills required by the company in the future will have a different emphasis and will stress cooperation and leadership rather than confrontation and control. The company believes that it is a mistake to think that creativity and effective management do not sit alongside each other. It would appear that successful creativity requires, above all, the application of basic techniques of management to solving business problems and opportunities. The new challenge for ICL Fujitsu is to create a corporate culture that allows all employees to be creative, not just the people involved in new product/service development projects. The company hopes that in the future everyone will take calculated risks, innovate, and show a display of courage and individualism that enables creativity to thrive. The attributes of individuals are seen as being as important to the future success of the company as short-term gains in productivity or operational efficiency.

The traditional company person

The key characteristics of the creative person needed by ICL Fujitsu in the future will differ from the conventional view of the 'company person' promoted in organizational mythology. The creative person will have to show the following traits:

- tolerate ambiguous situations and know when to shape environments and when to leave them;

- prefer autonomy and freedom in everyday decision-making and find out what they love to do;

- enjoy taking calculated risks and have a strong wish to take sensible risks in any organizational setting;

- adapt to change and think positively about the long term management/strategy of the business;

- lower the need for support and have the ability to reconceptualize intractable problems;

- resist conformity and have a strong desire to overcome obstacles and not let problems overcome the individual.

These attributes are welcome in the company but problems have been identified, particularly in the areas of communication and delegation. Many of these attributes are required by the company and could be the foundations of an effective empowerment programme. The high tolerance of ambiguity is an advantage to a company that is being faced with constant change. Another character trait evident in creative individuals is a feeling of inner strength, a belief that they will endure, no matter what trials and tribulations arise in their everyday activities. This ability to cope, particularly with the increasing pace of change, is the variable which differentiates ICL Fujitsu individuals from many other company's employees. They tend to be self-assured and exhibit a high level of creative energy, which builds the foundations on which their creative and business skills are developed.

Creativity is risky, difficult to manage and expensive. To be truly creative, companies must stick their necks out on untried products and services, not knowing if they will be a success or not. They have to try to manage creative people, who tend to be non-conformist and anti-authoritarian and most of whom will rapidly become dissatisfied and choose to leave the company if their needs are not fully met.

Strategists need to recognize that not everyone will desire to be creative and that there are often few devotees of the creative message. Creativity will not just happen, and the selection process is the first opportunity to balance the need for creative energy with the desire of the majority of employees for caution and common sense. This point is important but it does not mean that your company cannot be creative. The 3M corporation is widely acknowledged as an innovative success story, producing a consistent range of new products to appeal to the global marketplace. The company has developed a corporate culture which can facilitate creativity and innovation, and employee turnover is virtually non-existent. Perhaps this can lead us to believe that the stability that is developed by the company allows it to meet the natural needs of the majority of people for caution and common sense, and to provide the foundations and impetus for innovation and creativity to take place.

Selection concepts considered in building creative companies

The building of selection systems will start with an understanding of the selection systems currently in operation within the company. These systems will have to be reviewed and improved, but they may well have been effective in the past and there is no reason to believe that they will not be effective in the future. The selection system will need to be supported by a series of activities that enable strategy to be integrated into the concept behind the process of selection. To assist this process the strategist should understand the issues surrounding the demand for and supply of creative people, potential improvements that could be made to recruitment procedures and the consistent development of the creative competencies needed by the company for its future success.

This success will not be automatic and is based on a clear understanding of the corporate issues outlined below.

Integrating business and selection strategies

A clear understanding has to be gained of the overall direction of the company and future human resource needs. The skills required are a key aspect: company restructuring, product development, new technology, cultural change or quality issues. The selection strategy used by the company is only in place to support the creative and business development aspirations of the company.

Implementing a resourcing strategy

The implementation of a resourcing strategy will complement the selection strategy of the company and will enable the creative company to have a view on the demand for people and skills, the availability of people both internally and externally, and the planning of recruitment campaigns. Other aspects include the ease of movement of people throughout the company and the staff retention levels.

Understanding demand and supply pressures

The forecasts of demand and supply are important factors in assessing the selection needs of the creative company. The strategic plans of the company should provide information on the following areas:

- new product development;
- market development;

- launch of new ventures;

- culture change;

- transfer of activities;

- cost reductions;

- decentralization proposals;

- productivity improvements;

- company restructuring.

Understanding the internal market

It is important to understand and track the movement of people in the company. This requires a clear knowledge of the future creative needs of the business and how the management of people is likely to be affected by changes in strategic direction. Modelling systems can be devised which could review the effect of various creative strategies on the people needs of the company.

Monitoring the external market

An analysis of the external market has to be conducted on a local, regional, national and international level. The availability of people is now diverse, and people may be selected from any number of countries and sectors of the economy.

Implementing recruitment improvement strategies

The approach to recruitment involves obtaining a strategic fit between the needs of the company and the people who are joining the company. The creative culture can be reinforced by the company at this stage and a clear emphasis can be placed on the desire of the company to enhance commitment to creativity. The first requirement is to specify the competencies, attitudes and behaviours required of people within the company. The belief and value systems of the company develop from the actions of senior management, who must reinforce the creative culture through the recruitment strategy.

Understanding company creativity requirements

The requirements for people need to be analysed in some detail, which means assessing the company strategy, culture, management style and work environment as they affect the individuals required by the company. The creative requirements of the company may centre on business growth or regeneration, the development of a creative culture, values and norms of behaviour, and the management styles of the company leaders.

Matching the business strategy

The strategic direction of the company will affect the company structure and the type of individuals being selected. The individual chosen will have to match closely the business strategy of the company.

Development of creative competencies

In matching the business strategy to the selection process, a set of competencies will be expected of the new recruits to the company. These competencies are varied and are shown in Figure 4.2. They need to be matched by the appropriate knowledge and skills. The process of applying the knowledge and skills to creative actions is important as value is added to the company as a result of the creative contribution of the individual.

EXERCISE 11: The search for creative competencies

Examine your company to discover whether it possesses the creative competency traits shown in Figure 4.3.

	Existing traits	Required traits (future needs)
■ Positive thinking		
■ Tolerance of ambiguity		
■ Preference for autonomy		

FIGURE 4.2 The competency wheel

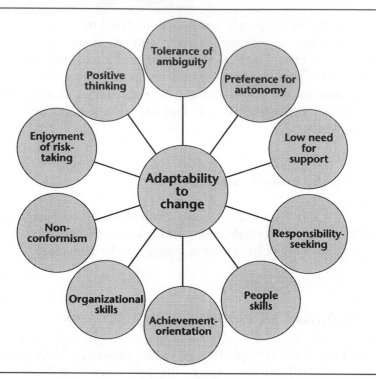

- Enjoyment of risk-taking
- Adaptability to change
- Low need for support
- Non-conformism
- Achievement-orientation
- Responsibility-seeking
- Organizational skills
- People skills

Now analyse the information you have:

- Are there any gaps in people requirements?

- How will your company manage the future people requirement gaps?

- Comments:

EXERCISE REVIEW

The gaps in people requirements will need an imaginative approach to be taken by the human resource management function of the business. A series of initiatives should be focused on the effective selection and integration of creative people into your company.

The selection processes of tomorrow will take their lead from the initiatives already being practised by leading companies. These approaches have become more complex in recent times, particularly with the strong emphasis being placed on testing procedures. The types of approaches used by companies vary quite substantially, and although their complexity has increased there is still a tendency to rely on the interviewing procedure as the final arbiter of the selection process.

Highlighted below are the range of approaches that may be chosen by companies to act as the foundation of their selection process.

Structured interview

The emphasis of the interview procedure must be on listening to the potential recruits' ideas on how they can ensure that a creative contribution is made to the company. The procedure has to be supported by a clear analysis of the competencies required to conduct the work. The focus will be on knowledge, skills and behaviour.

Questions will be structured to elicit information on the extent to which the person can make a creative contribution to the company. The answers provided by the candidate can then be assessed against a predetermined set of criteria which will be agreed at senior management level. The candidate should be given a series of situations which have been identified as critical to success in work performance. A typical interview session would involve the use of pre-prepared questions; using this technique, a reasonable assessment could be made of the candidate's creative potential.

Testing

Selection tests can provide an objective measurement of creative abilities and tendencies. The tests involve the application of standardized procedures to issues which enable the candidates' responses to be quantified. The differences in numerical scores can represent differences in abilities and behaviour. An effective test needs to be able to discriminate between people on the issues of sensitivity and has to be standardized and reliable. Behavioural norms can be established which will assist the company in achieving its strategic goals and building a creative culture.

Biographical information

The biographical information required by a company may focus on a candidate's education, previous creative successes, interests and career motivations. The basis of the process is job analysis, and the analysis of present people in creative positions can be utilized as a starting-point. Questionnaires and scoring systems can be developed for specific roles within the creative company.

Assessment centres

The assessment centre can be a very effective instrument in helping to identify development needs. The role of the centre could be to analyse the behaviour of creative people. Simulation exercises can be used to assess performance and these can be supported by tests and interviews. Interaction capabilities and creative competencies can be identified and tested, and observers can add weight to the conclusions of the assessment team. The methods outlined provide an excellent opportunity to assess the extent to which potential creative people match the culture of the company. Observing people in a series of situations will provide a clear indication of their behaviours in typical situations experienced by the company.

The assessment centre obviously has a two-way benefit because the company can allow the potential employee to assess the company as well. The assessment centre can help to support the selection process and can reinforce the decision-making of operational managers.

Selection is a golden opportunity for a company to build the foundations of the creative culture within the company. The opportunity to promote the creative culture of the company and communicate the values and expectations of the company and its senior management must not be missed by the human resource function.

This could be an opportunity for a strategist to develop new methods of selection which could complement the more traditional systems used by organizations. The selection approach of the future will be based around a more balanced and equitable view of the role that people play in the performance of their companies. Many potential employees will have to build a portfolio of creative skills and evidence of their involvement in a series of creative tasks to show a prospective employer, rather than a body of experience which will be quickly seen as out of date. This approach will be very similar to that of the actor or designer auditioning or canvassing for support for a series of new designs. In the creative world of the future the selection system will be firmly based on adding value to the future of the company and not on previous experience and time-serving. Pressure will be placed on prospective employees to utilize their future creative potential to convince potential employers that they can and will contribute to the long-term creative success of the company.

Criteria on which to select in a variety of companies

The criteria that companies will use to select the individuals who wish to join their organizations will focus on the following areas:

- discipline;
- initiative;
- value;
- challenge;
- vision.

Each company will have to base its choice of individual on a different set of factors. These will depend on the history of the company, the markets it occupies and its competitive strategy.

■ discipline: engineering/manufacturing focus.

■ initiative: new business based on offering client support and consultancy solutions.

■ value: utilization of all effort to reach high levels of productivity and success.

■ challenge: new product development/innovation process.

■ vision: independent action/team operations.

CASE OUTLINE: THE DISCIPLINED APPROACH TO CREATIVITY NEEDED BY RANK XEROX

The Team Excellence Awards used by Rank Xerox promote creativity within the company. A project is selected by a division of the company and the success of the project is judged on the basis of four key criteria:

1 Business results and impacts.

2 Quality processes and techniques.

3 Teamwork.

4 Innovation and creativity.

The success or otherwise of the team is based on these criteria and whether or not the team has been creative or innovative in the use of its processes and outputs. This approach ensures a disciplined approach to encouraging creativity within the company through the identification of creativity as a specific requirement of success in any team activity within the company. The use of the term creativity in this instance is only a starting-point in the operations of the company and could easily be extended to include aspects of quality, teamwork performance, business results and selection processes.

The question of creativity is reviewed on the basis of a judgement as to whether creativity requirements were met as verified by the customer or by representative groups of customers. It is also raised when examining the effective use of people within the project. An assessment can be made of the creativity of the team compared to the competition, and this could form the basis of an assessment procedure based on competitive benchmarking. Including creativity at the heart of the working processes of the company encourages managers to examine in greater detail the selection procedures that are supporting the system of creativity within the company. The emphasis within the company is strongly placed on the need for a disciplined approach to managing creative projects, particularly the need for cost-effectiveness at all times.

The success of Rank Xerox in recent times has been based on their clear understanding of the process of competitive benchmarking and quality. They have focused on the need to manage the financial pressures of each new product and this has led to the development of an efficient new product development process. The popularity/success of each new product produces its 'team stars', who are often in great demand throughout the company for similar or more complex new product development projects. The importance of quality is discussed with every new recruit to the company. An understanding of the financial discipline and quality standards is an important prerequisite for joining the company. This is high lighted in Table 4.1, where you can see the link between financial discipline and a strong focus on lower-cost products and creativity in keeping production costs to a minimum.

TABLE 4.1 Financial discipline in the creative process

Lower-cost products
- Processes
- Marketing
- Delivery

Creativity
- Lower costs
- Lower cycle times

EMPLOYEE AWARENESS
- What you have to do
- Roles and responsibilities
- Customer awareness – internal and external
- Focus on key deliverables

CASE OUTLINE: SOMEONE WHO CAN TAKE
INITIATIVE AND ACT

A different approach towards the selection process is being taken by many companies but is particularly prevalent in the technology sector, where an agile mind that can address individual customer needs is critical to the success of a company. The industry is driven by changing customer requirements and the ability to identify customer needs quickly and turn those needs into products and services that perhaps did not exist in the past. The need in the technology sector is for people who can act on their own initiative and understand the marketplace. The selection process takes into account the desires of the individual but also makes it clear to the prospective employee that this sector is experiencing rapid change.

The ability to take initiative and to act has to be tested at selection. This will require investment in assessment processes and a series of interviews with different levels of managers. The selection system for these companies will have to test the applicant's ability in the following key areas:

- entrepreneurial ability of the individual;

- networking skills;

- business planning skills;

- creative skills;

- resilence and determination;

- training needs.

The individuals working in this sector are selected on their ability to act as a business development specialist with a varied client base.

CASE OUTLINE: AN INDIVIDUAL WHO CAN ADD
REAL VALUE IN A SMALL BUSINESS

An individual that can add real value to a business can often be found in a small enterprise which is growing fast in a developing market. In many ways this type of company is experiencing a constant battle for survival and needs to improve the methods used to run the business at every opportunity. An example can be found in a rapidly growing small company which supplies a technology-based product and service to the retail sector in the UK. The company has to rely on the input of all levels of people within the company. The company is concentrating on the recruitment of people who can be individual thinkers with responsibility for running their own small section of the business.

The mission of the business is focused on the beliefs of the founding directors, who base the company culture on freedom to act and think with the absence of 'parental' control. People are expected to formulate their own solutions to work-related and customer problems. The concept is being explored by allowing individuals within the company to behave as owner-managers. The key problem faced by the company directors is how to structure decision-making to allow that freedom to flourish while maintaining control of financial resources. Supporting these beliefs is a hope that the vibrancy of the company and the attainment of corporate objectives can be fuelled by independent thinking and autonomous action throughout the company.

The selection procedure within the company is biased towards the need to direct people and not manage individuals. You should ensure that the people working with the company have a high level of trust in the competencies of senior management and a strong belief in the vision of the company. The selection system is based on a job specification and not a job description; this is decided upon by the company after an extensive process of deliberation by the senior management team.

The focus is on the development of project management skills throughout the company, so that in reality the company is employing people who can exercise the skills necessary to manage medium-sized projects. The skills necessary for task completion are important and when a task is outlined it can quickly be undertaken in a single-minded and determined way. Administrative skills are possessed by everyone in the company and a detailed understanding of management procedures is important. It is crucial to play an active role in the design of administrative procedures so that they are closely related to the operations of the business. Also vital is the ability to juggle a series of tasks and to manage a portfolio of work which is constantly changing.

CASE OUTLINE: EMPLOYEES WHO HAVE A STRONG DESIRE TO CHALLENGE AND QUESTION IN 3M

3M is a company which promotes a climate of innovation and creativity. The company underpins its creativity by selecting people who have excellent interpersonal skills and are prepared to use them to build an extensive network of contacts and relationships within the company. The company does not select people who exhibit traits of pomposity that may prevent them from communicating effectively with a variety of nationalities.

The 3M person is certainly not a maverick in the true sense of the word but is encouraged to act and to have a strong desire to challenge and question the status quo. The interpersonal skills of employees are important in the search for creativity within the company and those required must be clearly identified at the outset of the selection process. Additional skills required include:

- the ability to enjoy achievement;
- networking skills;
- enthusiasm in everything they do;
- challenging skills.

3M has a dual career ladder: one ladder is for management and the other honours the success of professional groups. The company provides a system that rewards people for their innovative abilities without forcing them into a management position where they may be unproductive.

The company does use some assessment methods to select people but it mainly relies on the interview process as an indicator of the success or otherwise of the candidate. The human resource function plays a key role in the selection and interviewing procedure at 3M and due consideration is given to the above skills when selection takes place.

Employee turnover across the company is very low and can only be recognized in the sales function of the company. This point may highlight the fact that corporate stability is required in order to build the foundations of creativity in a company. The stability of the company has to be marketed to the potential employee in an attractive and meaningful manner, so that the 3M employee is excited about the prospect of working for the company.

The company enjoys taking only calculated risks; this is often the approach of the lone entrepreneur in a small company who recognizes that one false move could dramatically affect the future of the business. Achieving balance in the selection of individuals who can carry the company forward into the next century is not an easy task and certainly the approach adopted by 3M in the past has worked very well.

CASE OUTLINE: PEOPLE WHO HAVE A CLEAR IDEA OF WHAT THEY WANT TO DO IN IMAGINATION

Imagination is a company which has very clear strategic objectives developed by the company founder and these objectives have a strong impact on the selection systems used by the company.[1] The company objectives have a direct link with the selection process in that the emphasis is based around one key question: what do you want to do? This is an interesting approach because it changes the whole nature of the selection process within the company. The emphasis in this company is different because the selection procedure is based on individual contribution and not on time-serving. The success of the selection process is evidenced by the age–responsibility ratio of many of the senior managers within the company. These managers are expected to formulate their own ideas on their level of contribution to the company and have a flexible and responsive approach to business management.

The company is prepared to provide career opportunities to young people if they exhibit the correct aptitudes and skills. This approach promotes a sense of cooperation throughout the company so that people assist in the completion of tasks efficiently and with creativity. This is a young company with interesting ideas on the personal creative contribution that can be made by everyone in the company. It expects everyone to do her or his creative duty (see Figure 4.3). The selection process is focused on the search for the following set of key attributes:

1   Shared and disciplined ownership of the completion of work. This is crucial to the success of the company.

2   Freedom and the search for creative solutions to problem-solving. Training is provided to support this process.

3   Clear understanding and the ability to work to constantly changing company objectives.

4   Identification of core tasks so that competencies can be clearly built.

5   Effective communication skills. These are used throughout the company.

6   The ability to assist people in experiencing activities which will have a direct effect on their behaviours.

7   The ability to become a total creative resource that can be made available to other areas of the company.

8   Understanding of business practice in order to develop an astute view of the business challenges facing the company.

9   Teamworking skills. These are enhanced on a regular basis.

FIGURE 4.3   The Imagination gateway

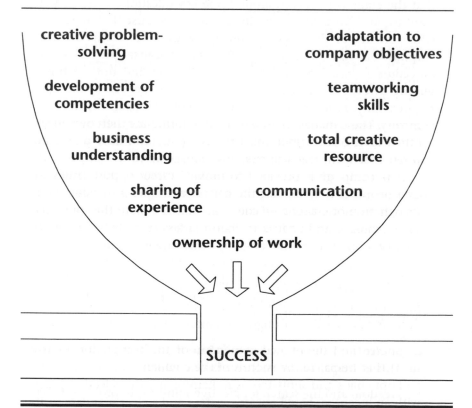

Corporate initiatives to support selection systems

To support the ideas outlined above a whole range of issues need to be explored by companies:

- *Excellence awards*: excellence awards are used by companies to enhance performance and improve the desire for achievement within the company. The use of excellence awards could also be extended to the selection procedure in that successful selection can lead to the award being given to line and senior management or perhaps individual functions inside the company.

- *Customer involvement*: customer involvement could be enhanced. If the creative employee is expected to work with the customer on a regular basis and develop a long-term and productive partnership, their involvement could be an effective method of assessment.

- *Benchmarking*: benchmarking could be an effective method of assessing the selection procedures utilized by companies and developing a view on their performance in comparison with existing methods. Competitive benchmarking can also be used effectively to compare directly the methods your company is using with the selection criteria of your competitors.

- *Training and development planning*: integrating the selection process into training and development plans is a key factor to consider when reviewing the selection procedures of your company. It is important to give people reassurance through the design and implementation of training and development plans that capture the imagination of creative people. You should ensure that their skills set is building and adding to their marketability in terms of your company and the general employment market.

- *Project-based portfolio of tasks*: these will include a range of projects that each person has contributed to in the past. This approach will focus the efforts of people on the need to achieve and develop their skills and knowledge through team interaction within the company.

- *Longevity*: the issue of longevity is important because the environment that helps creativity thrive is one which promotes longevity and not chaos and short-termism. Reinforcing the selection process with an incentive-based rewards system and a clear mandate to stay with the company, and applying a long-term and strategic approach to the creative process will be important in the creative company of the future.

The key attributes of the creative person are highlighted in Table 4.2. Once these attributes have been identified the individuals will have to be successfully integrated into the company. The traditional approach of the induction programme can be effectively supported by the training and development strategy of the company. The two aspects have to work in tandem to ensure that value can be added to the creative processes of the company as quickly as possible. Future approaches will include the following:

- a detailed description of the creative process taking place in the company;

- an explanation of why creativity is the lifeblood of the company;

- an assessment of the contribution that can be made by all groups of people within the company to the creative process;

- future developments and details of any idea forums used by the company;

- an explanation of the creative contract between the employee and the company.

TABLE 4.2 Key attributes of the creative person

- Communication skills
- Disciplined approach to responsibilities
- Ability to develop their own views on the marketplace
- Independent decision-making skills
- Initiative
- Networking skills
- Resilience and determination
- Independent administrative abilities
- Enjoyment of achievement

Re-examining the expectations of the company

The selection system can be an ideal opportunity to re-examine the expectations of the company and the individual, and to establish the foundations of a relationship between the company and the individual. The elements of the creative relationship can also be explained to each employee in order to agree the expectations of each party. Monitoring of progress against the expectations of the individual and the company should include the following aspects:

- An outline of company expectations: the expectations of the company in terms of creative output must be explained to the prospective employee so that a clear understanding exists between the individual and the company.

- Target-setting: this aspect would build on the company expectations in that targets could be agreed which would motivate each individual and assist the company in meeting strategic objectives.

- Agreed joint self-development strategies: at the outset of employ-ment with the company a joint development programme between the new recruit and the company could be agreed. The emphasis of the development programme would be on self-development and joint responsibility.

- Idea-generation success: the generation of new ideas will become the norm within the company. What is expected of each individual, the systems that are to be used and the rewards for effort should be made clear to the new recruit.

- Consistent review of individual expectations: the consistent review of each individual's expectations should be addressed at the outset of the relationship between the company and the individual.

- Training and development support: the self-development opportu-nities on offer throughout the company need to be published. The structure, systems and availability of training and development will be made clear to the new employee and a learning contract will be devised.

- Creativity opportunities for individuals and teams: the opportunity to be creative will be stressed to individuals, and the systems to be used will be fully explained to each new employee. The focus on team development and creativity will be outlined, and the methods used to motivate and manage team efforts will be discussed.

- Understanding of company reward and recognition systems: the link between rewards and recognition for individual, team and company effort should be explained.

CHAPTER FIVE

Developing creative people

This chapter will examine the importance of developing people as a source of creativity in the struggle to find a sustainable competitive advantage. The process of development can act as a springboard for creative thinking and a test bed for ideas on the most suitable approaches to be adopted in the creation of new management systems, products or services. Management development can offer you the opportunity to influence creative thinking in your company.

The development process in a creative company has to motivate senior management to take advantage of the solutions offered by a strategic approach. The development process has to be viewed as an integral part of the drive towards business development success and not as an add-on which can be avoided when creative solutions are not forthcoming.

You should train and develop employees to have an imaginative approach towards problem-solving in their own departments. Encourage employees to search for an appropriate solution to the operational problems affecting corporate performance. The aim should be to develop a set of employees who can focus on the skills needed to exhibit initiative and implement business development ideas throughout the company.

The development process can be used to take a strategic view of the strengths and weaknesses of the company and to support the ability of employees to spot business opportunities. Training and development are being utilized in companies to set standards and to reinforce individual behaviour. The role of the development specialist will be re-examined in this chapter. Matching the training and development strategy to the individual needs of employees is very important in the creative process. Promotion of self-development can assist the business development process. Building closer partnerships with suppliers and customers can enhance performance and create a more focused approach to service and product development.

Discussed here are the traditional methods of training and development and how these form the basis of your corporate approach to training and development.

The traditional methods will not be replaced; rather, the challenge is to build on the existing systems within your company. The design of an auditing system is an important task for many companies. The auditing system will allow the development function to get an excellent view of the business environment and enable you to conduct a detailed assessment of the corporate health of the training and development function.

The development unit may be changing dramatically in the future; examples of its changing role will include:

1   A company may decide to raise operational standards throughout the company in order to enhance customer service levels. On the achievement of those raised standards the next stage of the process will be to enable managers to develop business ideas independently from the central focus of the business.

2   The role of company troubleshooter may be taken on by the company's development specialist. This role may consist in clearly identifying business areas which require the attention of senior management. One such issue is the importance of creativity and the difficulty of placing creativity at the centre of development plans within the business.

3   Another key task is linking the training and development strategy of the company to the personal needs of individuals. If you can ensure that the personal needs of individuals are taken into consideration during development planning, the popularity of development can only grow within the company.

4   The fourth approach is to have a development unit which focuses on promoting self-development amongst key employee groups, with a strong emphasis on business development activities. The introduction of self-managed learning could underpin the business development process. The self-managed learning process is certainly applicable to companies that operate in a fast-moving business environment.

5   Use development as a method of building closer working partnerships with customers and suppliers to assist the development of new products and services. The sharing of information will be a key source of creativity between your company and your customers.

EXERCISE 12: Examine your own company

Let's examine some of the typical aspects to be found in any organization; while you are reading this section ask yourself if you recognize your organization. You may recognize many of the problems outlined below and you may witness a move away from the traditional methods of training and development in your company.

The traditional methods of development are still important and will form an integral part of the development process within the creative company. The traditional approaches include some of the following:

- a strong emphasis on training and skills development within your company;

- the focus of effort on the presentation and input of information into the annual training plan;

- the bureaucratic nature of the planning process and a strong focus on control and centralization in decision-making;

- the availability of training resources and internal competition, which results in an attempt to secure additional financing for individual projects through the budgeting system of the company;

- encouragement of internal competition because of the increased levels of efficiency that can result from direct competition over scarce corporate resources;

- detailed training needs assessments which will feed information up and down the corporate ladder and centre decision-making at the top of the company;

- the evaluation of training programmes by intelligent management who understand their position in the hierarchy and the effect their development programmes have on career development within the company;

- the design of learning events following a set pattern and the promotion of these programmes, managed from the centre of the business with an emphasis on the administrative success of the event;

- strict management of the corporate training budget which does not invite questioning from the management team.

■   Comments:

EXERCISE REVIEW

You may find that the foundations of an effective training and development function are already in place in your company. The function may require additional support from top management or it may need to be refocused towards the creative needs of the business.

The established methods have their place in modern companies, but one of the problems faced by the training and development function is how to take advantage of the popularity of development and make it an integrated part of the company philosophy. One method is to introduce an auditing system which can focus the company on the customer, the market, the individual and corporate capability. The aim of the development audit is to broaden the scope of training and development and to allow the function to take a clear view of the business environment. The audit will focus the attention of the development specialist on the needs of the company and increase the relevance of her or his activities to the creative teams operating in the company. It will focus on the ability of the training and development function to find, maintain and build a position of influence in the company. This position will allow them to have a strategic voice in the boardroom which can reconceptualize the future vision of development in the company. Finding this position depends on having the correct information on the internal and external challenges facing the business. A well-designed audit provides a basis on which top team discussions can be based.

Collecting and storing the information can be difficult and costly. Moreover, in times of rapid change, information only has a limited shelf life. Information will be available from many sources in the company and this will need to be matched by market and customer information. The auditing system will have to filter the information and capture the information necessary to provide the development function with a strategic voice.

Audit design

The design of the auditing system is crucial to the success of the development process within the company. It has four main factors which provide the basis for the design of the system.

Customer

Understanding the customer is fundamental to implementing a successful development strategy across a company. The customer can be an internal customer of a particular department, for example human resource management, or the external customer purchasing the product or service.

1   Who is the customer?

- size of the customer base;
- number and variety of customers;
- customer profiles.

2   What are the customer's needs and how are they changing?

- existing customer needs;
- changing nature of customer needs;
- future needs of customer groups.

3   Do needs match the product or service development process?

- analysing the product/service development process;
- integrating the process with an assessment of success;
- matching development needs to new innovation projects.

4   How can benchmarking be used in your company?

- competitive benchmarking;
- success stories and adoption by the company;
- gap analysis and competitive analysis.

5   How is the quality of the development service being assessed?

- standard-setting;
- focus groups and working with top teams;
- quality targets linked to employee development forecasts.

6   What are the performance achievements in creativity?

- increasing speed to market;
- improving the process of managing creativity;
- developing the product/service development project leader.

Market and the environment

Understanding the market and the business environment is fundamental to establishing the link between the impact of the development strategy and the bottom line performance of the business.

1   Does the political environment support the development process?

- existing/future level of government support for development;
- local government support;
- institutional initiatives.

2   How can the cultural impact of development initiatives be assessed?

- transnational project success;
- levels of cooperation achieved;
- use of international project teams.

3   Are you taking advantage of the technology available to reinforce the development process?

- establishment of network systems;
- use of information technology;
- use of communication systems.

4   Does your company have an intercompany development strategy?

- focusing on sharing information/development resources;
- building a structure that supports action and implementation;
- introducing development systems that can be applied across the borders of the company.

5   Do you understand the total market for your products and services?

- size and spread of the market;
- growth of market share and market presence;
- product/service positioning in a variety of markets.

6   How many new product/service development initiatives are taking place at the moment?

- new product/service targets that work;
- number and complexity of existing product/service initiatives;
- selection of initiatives against development needs.

7   Are you aware of the changes in the structure of your industry and the impact they have on your development strategy?

- new skills and knowledge;
- new corporate needs;
- industry standards – setting the pace.

8   Do changes in the profitability of your industry have an impact on development strategy?

- security of resource allocation in your company;
- security of support for development initiatives;
- new projects linked to the enhancement of performance.

Individual

The individual needs of people employed in the company have to be taken into consideration in constructing development strategies. The opportunities that are offered to each person will be a critical factor in motivating people towards creative activity. These needs have to be matched on a continuous basis to the creative objectives of the company.

1   Have you analysed the future career expectations of creative people?

- understanding the fragility of the career structure;
- managing career expectations;
- examining the role of development in the career process.

2   Do you update the knowledge and skills base of creative individuals?

- encouraging individuals' input into their knowledge/skills profile;
- promoting self-development projects;
- highlighting the provision of opportunity.

3   Do you assist people to develop creative thinking skills?

- ensuring that the creative techniques are available;
- providing thinking time to build the creative process of the company;
- giving management support to the initiators of creative projects.

4   Do you listen to the internal market for development needs?

- what listening posts do you use?
- do you use focus groups?
- what communication systems support this process?

5   Do you build your awareness of the creative needs of individuals within supplier and customer companies?

- presentations on development programmes/strategy;
- sharing of resources;
- cross-fertilization of creative teams.

6   Do you reward successful development initiatives?

- implementing recognition schemes;
- funding new development initiatives;
- building a hierarchy of development awards for indivduals, groups and business units.

Corporate capability

The capability of the company to respond to the changing nature of the business environment is an important factor to consider when introducing development strategies to enhance the creative process within a company. Corporate capability can manifest itself in several areas of company activities, including:

1   The creative marketing capabilities of the company:

- creative marketing strategies;
- internal marketing: marketing skills and knowledge;
- creative marketing orientation.

2   The creative capabilities of the company sales teams:

- adoption of new selling techniques;
- idea-generation techniques and targets;
- creativity in the design of management systems.

3   The development of strategic capability in innovation skills among senior managers:

- introducing senior management workshops;
- introducing individual skills programmes;
- coaching and mentoring in creative skills.

4   Creative team-building skills throughout the company:

- making new team-building ideas accessible;
- promoting team-building skills;
- linking successful teams and learning from success.

5   Business development skills among business unit managers:

- measuring skills and performance;
- ensuring uniformity of approach to development;
- redefining business development skills.

6   Support for the new product/service development process:

- identifying product/service development managers' needs;
- working alongside the managers in product/service development;
- meeting new needs and demands.

7   Construction of interpersonal development programmes in the company:

- building existing and future capability;
- sharing ideas and concepts;
- building communication networks.

The purpose of the development audit is to enable relevant and informed discussions to take place between the development specialists and the business strategists. These discussions will lay the foundations of the development strategy and ensure that the development strategy becomes an integral part of the vision and values of the business. The integration of development into the vision statement will assist managers throughout the company to focus on improving the internal effectiveness of the operational aspects of development and enhance the entrepreneurial activities of the business. The values need to be quite specific and the enhancement of creative activity within the company must be viewed as a key corporate objective of the senior management team.

The need for creativity has to be clearly stated by the strategic leader of the company if employees are to take their lead from the top team. These values have to be supported by a series of activities, systems and incentives to reinforce the need for continuous development.

The audit in practice

The development audit will assist you in placing your company among the increasing number of organizations that have developed their employees to use creative processes and systems. It is important to promote and encourage their use at every opportunity. The use of development techniques can be very profitable and can reinforce the search for success in your company. In order to support the implementation of a new development strategy the following factors are important.

Strategic leadership

The development audit should be given top priority by senior management. The vision of the company should be based on a creative company culture supported by a diverse range of development opportunities for every employee. The role of the human resource manager will be to market her or his development strategy throughout the company and to ensure that the strategy is kept as relevant to current business needs as possible. The senior management team will be the most effective marketing tool for the development strategy.

Implementing the development audit

Strong links need to be developed between human resource managers and the strategic planners within the company. The audit has to be viewed as dynamic and relevant to the business. The results of the audit must be openly discussed within the senior management team if they are to be seen as an important part of the strategic planning process.

Scanning the market

Scanning the market is crucial to the success of a development audit. The creative company needs to be ahead of the competition in utilizing the development methods available. The development strategy has to be externally focused to enable the organization to integrate new approaches into the strategic thinking of the company.

Linking strategy to operations

The development strategy has to be shown to have a real impact on the success of operational activities within the company. Companies need to develop methods of reviewing the success of development activities at the operational level. Questionnaires directed at the customer and the operations function can be used to determine the effect of the development strategy on the everyday activities of the business.

Competitive advantage through new thinking

New thinking is needed in the area of linking creative actions to the development strategies of companies. Development can be an effective method of enhancing corporate competitiveness and promoting a culture of business achievement within the company. The successful implementation of a development strategy is as an important stage in the pursuit of competitiveness. Once an organization has established a series of operational standards, these can be supported by the introduction of a development strategy aimed at corporate creativity.

The ownership of individual development can act as a powerful method of ensuring that the role of the development adviser is strategic in nature. Promoting a personal desire for achievement throughout the company can act as a process of *pull-through* in terms of increasing demand for development opportunities. Self-development is increasingly important as a method of building competitive advantage, as employees aim to develop new business by working closely with customers. The new strategic thinking can be seen in the following leading companies: Whitbread, Motorola, Leo Burnett and ICL Fujitsu.

CASE OUTLINE: WHITBREAD COMPANY

Enhanced creativity through development opportunities is seen as the next stage of company competitiveness. The strategy adopted includes a link between several areas of company operations.

The recognition that standards have to be improved in all areas of the business before real improvements in overall corporate performance can be achieved is an important foundation of the business development plans of the company. Underpinning the need to raise standards was a strong desire to improve quality within the company. A supporting mechanism for any improvements was the use of detailed development strategies.

The skills of the Director of Human Resources were critical to the successful implementation of new business development plans and the achievement of higher levels of creativity within the company. The skills required included the need for a clear focus on the role of human resource management. The role had to be accepted at a strategic level if it was to be successful in supporting the creative process. The determination and resolve of the Director is crucial to the success of the development strategy in any company.

The improvements are based on a points system, which recognizes the importance of business development and links it to the need for business improvements across the group. Achieving improvements was not easy, and progress was fragmented at times. Measurement is important, and this involved establishing a points sytem within the various outlets in the company. Measurement was supported by an achievement system which gave a gold star to the outlets which achieved high standards of quality and service. The attainment of the gold star was difficult, and a great deal of enterprise had to be shown to achieve it. The use of measurement techniques is an effective method of raising standards but can also be the first stage in improving levels of business development. Once high levels of quality have been achieved, a company can start to look at the different techniques for improvement in creativity and, ultimately, business performance.

The aim is to develop a company culture based on *winning* behaviour. Creativity is actively encouraged in the company and the opportunity is now being given to employees to write their own standards and to set their own forms of measurements and targets. The next stage could be for the company to explore an internal set of quality measures based on levels of creativity and the effectiveness of innovations introduced throughout the company.

A new mode of thinking has been adopted by the management team of the company which recognizes creativity as an important issue and one which needs a high level of commitment to ensure that it takes place.[1]

CASE OUTLINE: MOTOROLA

The role of the creative development consultant is emerging in Motorola and is based around efforts in the company to change the traditional thinking within the company. It centres on the following issues:

- inventing new development processes;

- utilizing innovative development approaches;

- engendering a constant pressure for learning in the company;

- becoming a development advocate;

- promoting a new mind set within the company concerning development.

The change in emphasis is away from control and towards freedom of thinking and action. One method used by the company involves the setting up of total customer satisfaction teams, which consist of a group of volunteers operating on a team basis. The aim is to enhance customer service and satisfaction through creativity, improved problem-solving abilities and new working systems. The new ideas introduced by the teams help to define company standards.

An outdoor development initiative has also been introduced to build the cohesiveness of the customer satisfaction teams.[2] This idea has involved the establishment of a development initiative designed around an intelligent learning approach to outdoor development. The development initiative will focus on the team members achieving a set of tasks through group work and intelligent problem-solving. The difference between this approach and previous methods used by the company is that the focus is on one new product development team at a time, and on a series of exercises which promote thinking and not physical achievement.

The aim of the company was to develop the following management competencies through the use of outdoor development:

- initiative;

- creativity;

- strategic visioning;

- managing uncertainty;

- controlling stress;

- attention to detail;

- tenacity;

- risk management;

- problem analysis.

The following factors were considered during the design period:

1   Search-and-find exercises could be used to develop team working, coordination and planning skills.

2   Survey exercises could be used to develop creativity, initiative and problem analysis.

3   Major management tasks could be used to develop creativity, tenacity and stress control skills.

These factors were influenced by time constraints and penalties would be awarded for non-completion of tasks. Definitions of the competencies were agreed with the participants and their managers at the outset of the initiative.

Review systems can be encouraged which will form a major part of the assessment process. A points system could be used whereby teams gain points based on the following criteria:

- achievement of task (30 per cent);

- effective process (40 per cent);

- effectiveness of review process (30 per cent).

The Motorola strategy is to focus on the process, so that the teams involved can centre on the *how* and not on the task itself. The points system can be used to benchmark the performance of different groups in the same organization and performance can be compared across business units.

This is a new and powerful way of developing creative people in a company. The focus of the initiative is on designing the outdoor events around specific competencies as defined by the management teams in the organization. The development method is dynamic and the focus is on what you do and on what you say.

In order for creativity to establish itself in the company the ownership of individual development needs is promoted. The importance of development and its link with creativity is evident in the business objectives of the company. This is reinforced by the company appraisal system and the development planning process. There is also a link between strategy at regional and international level and the development and creativity needs of local sites.

Annual succession planning is used to identify high-potential people in the company and to assess the creative skills needed for the future success of the business. The level of creative skills in the company is measured, and good and bad practice are identified at the development centres used by the company. Group assessment is used to measure the relevant creative behaviours required by the company. The company identifies the following key factors during assessment:

- creative leaders;

- creative teams;

- creative stimulants for action;

- components of the creative environment;

- consensus regarding development needs for future success.

The role of creative development consultant is evolving within the company; this person will actively assist managers in the introduction of creative ideas and new products into the market-place. A consultancy role has recently been undertaken by the company training function during the development of a new product for the European market. The product manager of the new product development project contacted the development consultant to discuss the use of a strategy workshop which could enhance the effectiveness of the team. The workshop was a great success and assisted the team in focusing on a clear product definition for the project and on building an effective team. The concept of placing marketing and business planning alongside development is now considered to be crucial to the success of new product development in the company.

The objective of the strategy workshops was to reduce the company's product development cycle times. The integration of four key factors enabled the company to lower the product development cycle times for a group of new products: product planning, development, feasiblity studies and team-building. The new product development process involved many of the key professional groups, including software and hardware engineers, tooling and moulding experts, mechanical design, distribution, finance, manufacturing, test and operations. The workshop had the specfic aims of speeding up the process of creativity, of focusing the attention of the team on key issues and of enabling a cohesive approach to develop within the team. Ownership of the new product was secured and the individual team members started to develop during the workshops.

Various skills were enhanced, including the technical aware-ness required to execute the project, general management skills, marketing and sales, market understanding, negotiating skills, interpersonal and decision-making skills. Other spinoffs from the success of the workshops are the enhanced motivation, excitement and involvement of everyone connected with the new product development process.

CASE OUTLINE: LEO BURNETT

The view that creativity can be enhanced through the personal desire for achievement is strongly held by this advertising agency. Management has recognized the strategic power of people develop-ment as a method of enhancing the creative process. A development programme has been introduced into the company and this has enabled the company to support the creative process and to achieve its corporate objectives. The programme is built around one clear concept: what helps people helps business.

The company places great emphasis on development and recognizes that the vision of the company will not be achieved without a healthy investment in development. The company has a clear strategy for producing more and better ideas, using the team concept and breaking down barriers at all levels of the business. It is now being recognized that learning within the company needs to be ongoing and dynamic.

The company recognizes the importance of on-the-job development and views it as the best method of learning about the creative process. This initiative is supported by formal development programmes at all levels of the company. The aim is to assist people in developing an individual repertoire of skills and to prepare them for new responsibilities.

The company works with individuals to eliminate their weaknesses and to build their strengths through regular and formal evaluations. These evaluations are based on the individuals' ability to develop and deliver new ideas and concepts. The development programme is based on an open learning approach which has proved to be successful; it contains a series of development modules which are perceived as important in the initial creative process:

- focus on time;

- presentation of ideas;

- managing creative people;

- marketing new ideas and concepts;

- competing in a changing world;

- industry-specific skills;

- strategic management in practice.

The company has recognized the importance of development and how it can be utilized in the search for a creative response to a changing marketplace. The problem the company is now experiencing is the high level of demand for development opportunites among its creative people.

CASE OUTLINE: ICL FUJITSU

Self-managed learning has emerged as a convincing and effective method of building new business and generating new ideas within this company. The concept is quite novel and has established its popularity in high-technology companies as an effective method of development.

It is essentially a creative approach to learning and is based around the concept of the customer leading the development needs of the company. It centres on building individual knowledge, skills and new attitudes towards development throughout the company. Each team consists of volunteers, who have identified a specific development need in an area of business, career planning, interpersonal skills, new knowledge requirements, negotiation techniques or the effects of organizational change. In practice, the team forms after attending a short workshop, which serves two purposes:

1   To brief the attendees on corporate business development issues.

2   To provide people with the skills required to establish an individual learning contract.

Once this process has been undertaken, support and challenge groups are formed with the intention of meeting every two months to identify progress against development objectives contained within an individual learning contract.

An effective group is one which has an active development plan, and contains individuals who accept responsibility for the following points:

- their own development;

- taking an holistic view of the company;

- building good facilitation skills;

- learning from experience and change.

The fundamental shift that has taken place in the company is that individuals recognize that development is their responsibility. If individuals can recognize this basic shift in thinking they can serve as business development consultants in the marketplace.

One simple question has to be asked by the company strategist: are we developing tomorrow's creative assets? If the answer to the question is positive, the next thought could be: are there any new methods that could be used to enhance corporate creativity and how are we monitoring the success or otherwise of the methods we are using at the moment?

Creativity can be enhanced by using various methods of development but support from the top of the company is clearly required, as is time to complete the development opportunities. The methods range

FIGURE 5.1   The result of placing people at the centre of creativity

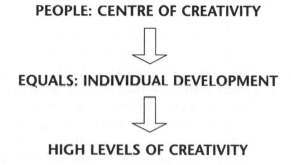

PEOPLE: CENTRE OF CREATIVITY

EQUALS: INDIVIDUAL DEVELOPMENT

HIGH LEVELS OF CREATIVITY

FIGURE 5.2   Competitive advantage through development model

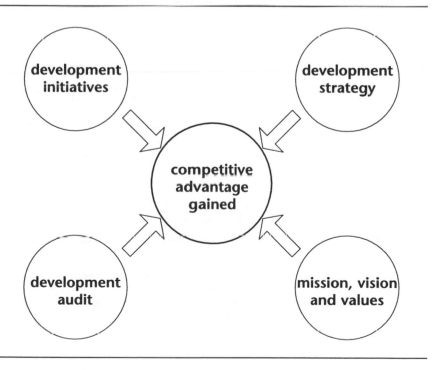

from consultancy-style advice, the development of strategies and development plans, self-managed learning, raising standards of creativity through development and recognizing people's individual creative needs.

Companies are poised to take advantage of the emergence of the development consultant. The consultant can work alongside the business development process and add real value to controlling the time to market and improving the effectiveness of the development process (see Figure 5.1).

The final case is one where the personal needs of individuals are highlighted and the development support is given by means of a group structure which enables old thinking to be challenged and new ideas to emerge. This is perceived as a creative approach to learning and enables new concepts concerning development to be considered by the company. Individuals can examine what value they actually bring to the business.

The aim of the company is to *combine creativity with practical thinking* in the pursuit of business development. This is the objective of any development technique associated with creativity. The development strategy has to be adding real value to the success of the business and not intervening in the effective running of the company. People development can have a strong impact on the bottom line of any business operation and a variety of approaches can be used to secure competitive advantage for your company (see Figure 5.2).

CHAPTER SIX

Rewarding creative activity

The introduction of creativity into a company is not easy, and although the seeds of the creative culture may exist, actions have to be reinforced on a continuous basis. The management of creativity requires a strategy supported by a reward system which recognizes creative behaviours. This presents a company with a unique challenge to design reward and recognition sytems that provide incentives not only for sales and marketing teams but also for development teams working on new products and the frontline people who interact with the customer.

Creative individuals have strong personal growth needs and are most productive in roles which generate high levels of motivation. These roles need to enable individuals to feel a degree of meaningfulness, a belief that they have some freedom of action and that their work activities provide feedback and therefore tangible results. Each role has to provide task variety, which requires a number of different skills and talents. The outcome of work has to be viewed as significant and as having a substantial impact on the work of others in the organization. Freedom does not mean autonomy, but independence and the use of discretion in the scheduling of work, and having an input into the methods used to carry it out.

This chapter will investigate the issues involved in the introduction of pay structures that reflect the flexibility required by today's organizations in meeting the changing needs of the marketplace. The pay structure will act as a method of undertaking a review of the creative process which exists in the company.

Another key issue to explore will be the area of *competency building* in the creative organizations of tomorrow. A great deal of work is taking place in a range of organizations from building societies to manufacturing companies in an attempt to develop a set of expected competencies. These competencies can apply to individual employees or work teams and are linked to the strategic goals of the company. A competency can be built in creativity and innovation. The reward and recognition system of the company is required to assist the development of the creative drive of the business. The reward and recognition system needs to support the efforts being made by the customer-facing employees to focus on the key activities of business development. The competency-based approach is only another method of rewarding and building the creative skills of the business.

The aim of a successful reward and recognition system is to produce behaviours in the people involved in the creative process which include:

1   Personal competence:

- building competency in your chosen task;
- instilling belief in yourself;
- matching skills/knowledge to the task.

2   Personal accomplishment:

- searching for personal achievement;
- aiming for a balance between personal/career achievements;
- promoting incentives to achieve.

3   Growth and development:

- focusing on self-development;
- understanding personal characteristics;
- matching growth and development targets.

4   Responsibility:

- encouraging the exercise of responsibility;
- developing mature thinking;
- understanding the importance of responsibility.

5   Personal freedom:

- making effective decisions;
- developing communication networks;
- promoting the sharing of information.

These aspects have to be seriously addressed when the design of a reward and recognition system is being considered, particularly when many of the creative people the systems are attempting to motivate are searching for freedom of action in their daily tasks.

The reward and recognition systems that are being used by a variety of companies are attempting to address an issue which has become increasingly difficult in recent years. Many companies have rationalized their operations on a radical scale, which has necessitated the removal of large numbers of people in middle management. Consequently, the morale and motivation of people are low, and the challenge of raising confidence and excitement rests with the company's senior management team.

The reward system has become an integral part of a corporate strategy and most systems will attempt to focus on the encouragement of people and the securing of high levels of commitment to the corporate culture. The reward system will support and develop work flexibility, creativity and innovation in every aspect of the company.

The creative reward system

Many companies are experimenting with new reward and recognition systems in order to add an additional incentive to organizational activities, and there are a series of successes in different sectors of the economy. The new ideas range from altering the career structure in technical and sales areas of the company to reflect an increased level of flexibility, through the introduction of new roles for personnel interaction with the customer, to the construction of competency-based reward systems throughout a company.

The reward system can act as the means of implementing the creative process in a company. It can be a significant method of ensuring success and must not be underestimated by the senior management team. The reward system used by a company has to reflect the *interdependence* of the five key elements which form the axis on which an effective reward system can be built (see Figure 6.1). These five elements work together to build the foundations of an effective reward system and to develop a creative corporate culture. An awareness of the importance of the customer is central to the reward system, to a close match between the market/business development opportunities, and to the corporate structure and systems of the company.

Organizational development

The structure of the company should be reviewed on a consistent basis. This review would form the foundations of discussion between the senior

FIGURE 6.1   Foundations of an effective reward system

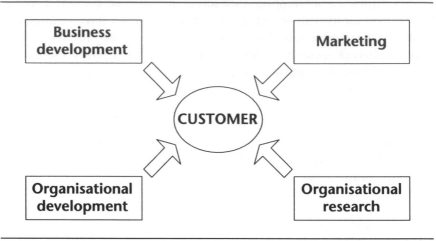

management team, the functional heads of the company and the strategist. The structure of the company will eventually be affected by the actions of the marketplace; this approach provides the strategist with an opportunity to lead the discussion and consider the outcomes of analysis of the future structure of the company and the effect it may have on the company's creativity. The creative momentum within the company can be maintained only if the company has a system which supports creativity where it really matters: in providing the product or service to the customer.

The organizational development of the company should focus on the innovation process and how creativity can be generated more effectively. This may result in a different structure emerging in the company, perhaps a team-based approach with a flatter corporate structure to encourage positive communication between employees. A network may be introduced which could ask individuals internal, or even external, to the company to comment on new products/services. The reward system may be difficult to design because of the problems of apportioning a monetary value to the generation in one part of the business of ideas which could be used in a different part.

Business development

The business development function of a company is often viewed as either the generator of sales or the negotiator of major acquisitions or mergers. It needs to be seen as a function in the company that promotes success through the design of an incentive-based corporate culture. Incentives should be provided to employees who have a direct responsibility for developing business and translating customer ideas into profitable products and services. These incentives could be monetary incentives, but recognition of expertise is also very welcome. The advice that the business development function can promote may prove invaluable in securing future sales and business success for the company. The business development function is in a unique position to advise the strategist and the human resource specialist on the most appropriate reward system for your company.

The strategist can take an independent view of the effect of a reward and recognition system on the motivation and morale of the frontline people in the business development process. The frontline people have to be motivated towards spotting business opportunities and working with the customer to turn those ideas into reality. The frontline employee will have a strong input into the design and implementation system that directly affects the everyday activities of this core group of employees.

Marketing

The marketing function will have a more hands-on approach to incentives than the business development function of the company. The sales function will be held responsible for direct sales, and the ability to be creative in the selling methods used by companies is often crucial to success. The marketing planning function will be working closely to add their views on the best selling methods. The role of the strategist can be to provide innovative ideas on individual and group rewards aimed at enhancing profitability and market share. The focus of many companies on market development can only fuel the drive towards introducing incentives/rewards which support the need for success in many companies.

Development of new business will have to receive a higher level of focus in many companies and indeed the need to reward this effort will become more important in the future. The new skills required by the salespeople of the company will alter the behaviour of the sales teams. The new behaviour will concentrate on developing consultancy-style skills which promote the advisory role of the salespeople. Direct selling will be important but the focus will change quite dramatically as the customer demands a more customized approach to customer–client relationships.

Organizational research

The strategist can use the techniques of organizational research to provide information and support for her or his arguments to change the reward and recognition systems within a company in order to enhance creativity. Research can initially be based on the attitude of people within the company to the present systems and suggestions for improvements. Attitude surveys can be taken on a quarterly basis, with a more detailed assessment being conducted on an annual basis. The survey results will only gain credibility if the strategist can turn the information into action. The research can act as a process to take the temperature of the company with regard to the effect of the present systems on the creative process. Later surveys can analyse the effect of the new reward and recognition system on the market, customer and competition.

The creative company can monitor performance through the use of competitive benchmarking with the objective of achieving best practice in its sector of the economy. This research could extend to the supplier network and the customer base, which will help to establish working partnerships which can enhance the creative process within the company by utilizing and sharing information.

Reward strategy modelling can be used to support the strategic decision-making in your company. The focus will be on scenario planning and on developing positive models and not negative down-sizing exercises.

This organizational research can assist you in developing a series of critical success factors which will form the foundations of your reward strategy. Once the objectives have been agreed, this will concentrate the minds of creative individuals on achieving success through innovation.

Customer

The internal customer is the focal point of activities aimed at improving creativity. Constant information is required by a company to understand the affect their incentives have on satisfaction levels throughout the company. This assessment of satisfaction is a continual process which has to be effectively managed by the strategists in the company. The examination of customer satisfaction will review the impact of the behaviour of service providers on the performance of the company. Customer satisfaction can be linked to the set of customer benefits you can offer and the creative process that can provide those benefits.

In order to change or alter behaviour so that customer satisfaction is achieved, a rewards and recognition package can be developed which has as its basis a set of service achievements which can have a direct impact on the reward package offered to the service providers. The effective monitoring of information in a creative company can lead to an improved level of customer service.

High levels of service give rise to high sales figures, which in turn attract more investment in new products/services from the financial decision-makers within the company. This investment would create a virtuous circle of increased attention to customer service and to the systems and structures that support the process of continuous improvement.

Many companies are experimenting with new reward and recognition systems which add *flexibility* and *responsiveness* to their competitive weapons. This flexibility is aimed at matching the changing nature of individual and corporate needs. There is a recognition that the reward strategy has to change to correspond to changes taking place in the business environment. This factor is the starting-point of many of the approaches being developed by European and multinational companies. A well-designed reward strategy will reinforce the business strategy and the search for creative success. The strategic leader of your company may become disappointed with the reward strategy if it has been designed to change gradually and does not adapt successfully to the changing nature of the business environment.

The typical reward system does not address the issues of creative behaviours very well. It is being recognized by strategists that a regular review of the reward system is necessary, so that it can assist rather than hinder the implementation of corporate objectives. Top management commitment is fundamental to the success of any reward strategy, and altering individual behaviour is recognized as being a key ingredient of success.

New approaches to reward and recognition

Companies are experimenting with a variety of reward and recognition systems in an attempt to enhance creativity and ultimately innovation. New approaches have to take into account that professionals, technologists, researchers, innovators and engineers may be motivated by monetary gain and not just the thrill of autonomy or the creative process. A new reward system is needed which integrates the financial and other non-intrinsic rewards with a new career structure for those key groups of individuals. The new approaches to reward and recognition are placing real pressure on companies to operate them successfully. The strategic objective of the reward and recognition systems (see Figure 6.2) may be one of the following:

- reorientation of functional groups of people in your company;

- the addition of incentives to the business development activities of your company;

- the development of a strong link between reward and recognition and the creative process in your company.

Reorientation of the sales team

The recent changes introduced at 3M show that the company recognizes that the sales teams need to react more flexibly to the needs of the business environment. The sales team has been reorganized along cross-functional

FIGURE 6.2   Strategic objectives of reward/recognition systems

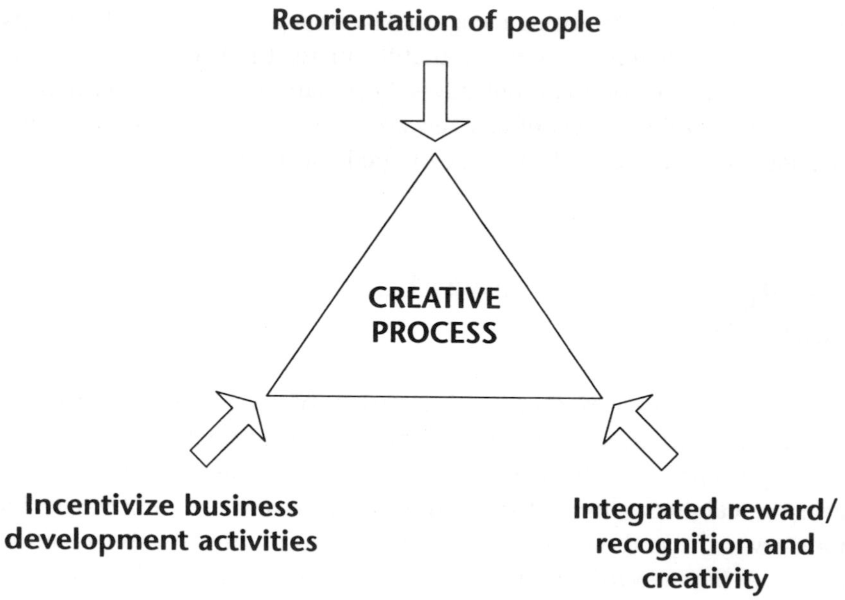

Reorientation of people

CREATIVE
PROCESS

Incentivize business development activities

Integrated reward/ recognition and creativity

lines and the achievements of each sales team are shared among the group. The aim is to link the payment structure and systems of the company to the performance of the individual and the group. This is a move away from the old-style rating system previously used in the company and has meant the introduction of a pay structure which reflects the need of the organization for a flexible response to the changing demands of it customer base. This new reward system was introduced with the desires of the sales team in mind, and by means of a close working partnership between the strategic planning function and line management.

The criteria for the reward and recognition system can be altered to fit the creative pressures that the company is facing. The new system can also highlight the individual efforts of salespeople.

The reward and recognition system, in this instance, is linked to the desire within the company to offer a new set of career opportunities to the sales teams. The company has been able to request increases in the levels of sales effort in the past and the sales teams have responded very positively to these initiatives. The company also recognizes that the organizational structure and creative dynamism of the sales team will be affected by an unsuitable system of incentives and rewards.

A comprehensive range of customer surveys is used to enable the company to respond to changing customer needs. The customer surveys also enable the strategists to identify human resource issues which can assist the sales effort of the company and help it to achieve its predefined targets, as well as allowing them to review the support the company provides for the sales team in terms of technical advice and training and development opportunities. 3M is developing a system which rewards employees for their creative abilities without forcing them into an administrative straitjacket which would frustrate and demotivate them.

The design of the rewards and recognition system has also taken into consideration the need for a constant flow of ideas into the company's product development departments. This requires that the reward and recognition system is closely linked to the company's idea-generation systems. In support of the new reward and recognition systems that are being used by the company, quality groups are used to focus specifically on creativity as an issue for the sales team.

Building incentives into business development activities

Rank Xerox builds incentives into the business development activities of the company and these are established with the cooperation of the marketing team. These rewards are cascaded down the various teams which form the new product development process in the company. The implementation of the business development strategy is critical to the success of the company. The company has a reward system which encourages the integration of ideas and cooperation between a series of teams which are directly concerned with the business development process. Examples of the incentives used by the company are:

- a bonus system which offers 5 per cent of salary to four levels of people in the company;

- a bonus system of 10 per cent of salary for all other levels;

- a bonus system of anything up to 30 per cent for directors in the company.

The incentives are designed to promote freedom of action in the pursuit of improved productivity throughout the company. This freedom of action is supported by three factors, as outlined in Figure 6.3. Objective-setting is critical to the reward strategy of the company and the achievement of corporate goals. It has been pioneered in the UK, where objectives are set each month to ensure the successful management of tasks throughout the company.

A disciplined approach to work is part of the training and development plan of the business and is strongly encouraged during

FIGURE 6.3 The focus of incentives

Freedom of action

Management Teams	Disciplined approach to work	Objective-setting and achievement

the induction period. A disciplined approach to work means that freedom of action can be encouraged with the full knowledge that consideration will be given to the manner in which work is conducted in the company. The management teams throughout the company are encouraged to focus on the effective management of resources and the need to structure work and to ensure its successful implementation.

Reward and recognition systems in the company are linked to success in productivity terms. The company clearly recognizes the efforts of individuals throughout the process. The functional managers in the company can allocate up to 1 per cent of their salary budget towards successful initiatives undertaken by employees within their function.

These initiatives have been supported by changes in the career structure, which provide the development teams with a new opportunity for recognition. There is an opportunity for the company to form a significant link between the creative process and the reward and career structures. This link can be secured only by active management of the reward system by the strategist and the human resource function. It is important to monitor of the effects of the reward system; changes can be made to ensure that the reward system remains on target.

Linking rewards and recognition to creativity

Leo Burnett is another example of a leading company developing a new approach towards reward and recognition. The company is developing systems that are linked to the development of creative freedom in the company. The view of the company is that the reward and recognition system helps to develop commitment, risk-taking and open communications throughout the organization.

Total commitment is expressed by the level of effort individuals will invest in working for the company. The reward system and the creative teams support risk-taking and this is evident in the fact that ideas can come from any level of employee in the corporate structure. The organization actively encourages the cross-fertilization of ideas and the exchange of information. The open-door policy extends from the senior management team down the corporate structure to the new graduate or recruit. This open-door communication was not always the case, and the company has made a determined effort to broaden the communications network of the company. An open-door policy is a prerequisite for creativity to take place in the company. The freedom given to each person is supported by a system of recognition and open access to senior management.

The reward system promotes individual potential, attention to detail, an understanding of the task, the skills to apply solutions to customer problems and a knowledge of who to work with in the company to achieve tasks. This provides the support which is required to discover solutions and consider the creative methods needed to implement them.

The financial systems used by the company have several key aspects: finance linked to activities, individual reports, independent reports against return on budget, and fiscal responsibilities. The financial systems can be linked to the creative process by utilizing the individual financial reports of the activities of each creative team and its leader. Independent reports against return on budget are introduced which acknowledge the need for financial discipline in the methods used to manage creativity. Fiscal responsibilities cascade through the corporate structure and this means that creative individuals can take responsibility for their own actions. Dealing with the failure of ideas or projects is viewed as an important part of the reward and recognition system at Leo Burnett. The important factor to consider in discussing failure in the organization is whether individuals actually learn from the process and the affect it has on future experimentation and risk-taking.

In Leo Burnett, promoting *initiative* is very important, and the reward systems have to be geared towards the achievement of this objective. The ability to take risks is a major factor in the success of the company, and the capacity to understand the customer's perspective and ask why some projects have failed and others succeeded must be recognized in the rewards system. The reward and recognition system can focus on the efforts of individuals and groups even if the project is a failure, so long as a high level of trust is maintained in the organization.

Recognition can take the form of a direct career opportunity for an individual, access to another project which interests the individual or the chance of presenting a set of ideas or new concepts to the senior management team. The reward and recognition system is viewed as a *dynamic process* which adds to the creative flair of the company and does not detract from the overall dynamism of the company. This is really the ultimate test of an effective reward system in operation: whether it adds to the creative energy of the company or detracts from it.

Key trends in leading companies

My research has involved a series of discussions with managers in 3M, Rank Xerox and Leo Burnett. They all recognize the importance of the reward and recognition system in meeting the needs of a creative company. It is accepted that there is a link between the corporate structure and the success of creativity, and that it is important to implement a reward strategy that meets the needs of a dynamic business environment. These companies have identified a series of trends that are changing their business operations and creating a drive towards a creative company culture based on a customer-responsive reward system:

1   Flatter organizational structures are encouraging experimentation in team-based approaches to the management of people. The use of network systems of communication can be an effective way of sharing creative energy and the outcomes of the endeavours of a series of teams across the company.

2   New professional career ladders are being introduced. Companies are having to recognize that the traditional methods of designing career structures are now under threat. In many organizations new thinking is required, which could result in more fragmentation of existing levels in companies or a recognition that promotion can only be managed in a horizontal manner rather than through the traditional vertical approach.

3   Objective-setting is complementing the reward systems of companies. The introduction of more clearly defined corporate objectives has led to a cascade effect in many companies. The achievement of corporate objectives is being realized through the monthly or quarterly objective-setting exercise taking place across business units.

4   New career opportunities are being introduced. The positive effect of many of these changes is that new career opportunities are developing in many companies. The traditional reliance on age and experience is gradually being replaced by the power of the idea, which can come from any source. This is particularly the case in the creative organization, where creativity may not have a direct link with experience. The service sector may also be affected by this trend, particularly in the case of new services which have only recently been launched into the market.

5   Responsiveness to the marketplace is being enhanced by reward systems. The weighting of many reward sytems is changing so that it is focused towards the customer and on securing new business development from effective client relationships. The emphasis is also changing in terms of the choice of the methods of reward or recognition used by the company. The choice favoured by the

particular employee group is an important factor to consider during the design of new methods.

6   Rewards systems are being used to support freedom of action, which is now paramount in many companies. Reward and recognition systems are being designed to support freedom of action, but also to reward and recognize initiative.

7   Focus groups are used to introduce new ideas on reward systems. The focus group is often used by the marketing function to test new products or services. The same principles are being used by leading companies to test the reaction of their employees to the new ideas on reward and recognition. This approach can pay dividends for companies if it is managed successfully, and it often works effectively if the services of an external advisor can be integrated into the process of implementation.

8   Reward and recognition systems are used to build flexibility, which is important at all levels in creative organizations. The reward and recognition system has to recognize the importance of the flexibility required to work across functions and to take on new skills and knowledge.

9   Flexible financial systems are linked to reward systems. This can involve the introduction of share options as part payment for the successful introduction of a new product or service. Allocation of benefits is often difficult to regulate because of the difficulty in apportioning rewards to individuals, teams, business units or the group as a whole.

10 Reward systems are being devised which provide commitment to creativity and support risk-taking. Competency-based reward systems which add to creativity can also reinforce commitment to the success of the business development process.

Lessons from the public sector

We have examined the approaches to reward and recognition systems which can be adopted by leading companies in the pursuit of creativity. An alternative viewpoint can be found by examining the approach to creativity adopted by employees and managers in the public sector of the economy. The public sector does not have the elaborate and flexible reward systems of some of the leading companies. The reward systems are often quite rigid and inflexible and certainly do not directly encourage creativity in many activities. For example, the pioneering work completed in individual projects in the health sector is certainly not motivated by direct financial rewards, but rather by a strong desire to achieve improvements in service. These achievements are often implemented against a background of very difficult organizational and political pressures.

One such project is a creative approach to community health care which has led the way in creative thinking on this health issue in the UK.[1] An innovative nursing team is established with a series of specific aims:

- to promote excellence in community practice;

- to identify standards of nursing care and ensure these are achieved by using a range of quality assurance methods;

- to explore and promote the full contribution of nursing to the multidisciplinary team;

- to motivate and facilitate the personal, professional and practice development of nurses themselves by providing educational opportunities and support;

- to provide a focus for research-based nursing and primary care development;

- to identify the key features of a Community Nursing Development Unit and to contribute to the development of the Nursing Development Unit project.

The creative team comprises district nurses, school nurses, health visitors, specialist nurses, support workers, a project nurse and a team manager. This creative team has been recognized as a central Nursing Development Unit for its innovative work in improving and developing community nursing. The award provides support over a three-year period for practitioner-led projects. The key aim of the creative team is to promote excellence in community practice. The creative team is a test bed for ideas and allows research and evaluation to be explored to their full potential as providers of high-quality health care.

The team commenced the project by conducting a brainstorming exercise which produced a detailed range of projects which required immediate attention. The enthusiasm for the project was high and the initial ideas were examined in detail and scaled down to a list of ten live projects. These were believed to be the realistic and achievable core initiatives and they became the basis for the nursing development programme. The projects selected were based on practitioner and customer priorities and built on existing development work. Key organizational, professional and governmental targets were incorporated into the the development programme.

The rewards received by individuals are not based around substantial financial incentives but, rather, on the desire for achievement and professional recognition:

- the opportunity to be involved in more challenging projects;

- immediate feedback on the success of creative efforts;

- national and international peer-group recognition;

- enhancement of professional standing;

- development of a passport to employability through skills development.

The success of this project is difficult to quantify and is not judged in financial terms but by the recognition that is given to the people involved in the project. This recognition can take the form of national awards, the allocation of individual study-time periods and career progression. The overall motivator is professional satisfaction and not financial reward. This could be an example for the future of reward and recognition schemes in the private sector. A reward and recognition strategy should be built around professional satisfaction and credibility and not financial rewards.

The second example involving the establishment of a creative idea through the motivation of individuals and not financial rewards is the setting up in London of a nurse-led specialist service for people suffering from anorexia nervosa. The establishment of any new service in the health sector is a formidable challenge for any innovator.

The task in the first year was to establish the Nursing Development Unit as a clinical service without any pre-existing service being in operation. The main issues to be tackled involved securing the position of the new unit with the key stakeholders, including the government investors, senior management, additional financiers; managing the service location; recruiting expertise; and strategy formulation and implementation. A quality and auditing system had been established in the organization as a way of enhancing quality of care. The main audit involved users in evaluating and designing the service and developing a clear strategy on the basis of this analysis. A vision of the future has now been established and a set of targets developed with the full involvement of unit employees and senior management sponsors of the project.

This project is a world leader and it has taken the inspiration of a handful of people to get it off the ground. The service has had to develop new methods of differentiating the offering to the customer in order to secure continuous funding of the project. This effort has been generated by a team of people who are not motivated by financial rewards but by the professional gratification they attain through the success of the venture. The incentive for people involved in the project comes from their individual motivation and belief in freedom of action. The key factor that motivates people involved with the project is the achievement of world leadership in an aspect of their professional life.

There are lessons that strategists can learn from the experiences of the health sector in attempting to manage the creative process and reward individual and team effort. You should:

- take advantage of a flexible reward system;

- focus on personal growth and achievement;

- aim for excellence through effort not money;

- build professional status through reward systems;

- recognize that enthusiasm can conquer perceived difficulties;

- link feedback to reward systems;

- promote international peer-group recognition;

- build a passport to employability by utilizing the reward system effectively;

- offer more challenging projects following successful completion of tasks;

- recognize that the overall motivator is professional satisfaction not financial reward.

Achieving balance in the design of a rewards and recognition system

We must accept the obvious lure of money as a key motivator but also understand that most individuals are often more interested in building their creative and professional standing. The creative company of the future will need to achieve a successful balance between these two factors, particularly when many companies are being designed as fragmented and flexible organizational structures.

Motivation is a difficult factor to analyse in any company because it is intangible. As creativity becomes more widespread in many organizations, the search to discover new ways of rewarding behaviour and building a climate of commitment and trust will begin. The focus of many companies may be on examining the motivations of creative teams rather than individuals, and on introducing systems that recognize the contribution of the individual as well as the group. The systems will have to take into account the network style of operating in many creative companies of the future and the isolation which tends to surround some creative people. The self-motivation often found in small enterprises could be introduced to promote a culture of achievement in the organizations of tomorrow.

The need for new ideas and concepts in this area of people management is crucial to creativity. There is a need for an objective view of how individuals are motivated, and the strategic planner is in an ideal position to take an informed view.

The creative organization of the future will set its own targets for new product and service development; this target-setting will be in

---

EXERCISE 13: Key questions in designing a reward/recognition system

There is a series of key questions to be considered during the design of reward and recognition systems for the creative company of the future:

1   Does your reward system build an achievement-based culture?

2   Do creative people respond positively to the present systems?

3   Does your present system reward personal effort?

4   How does the present system motivate creative people?

5   Do you recognize freedom of action in the company rewards system?

6   Do your customers have an input into the design of your reward and recognition systems?

7   Are you involved in research to support the development of your new systems?

8   Does the reward system support or hinder sales activities?

9   How do you encourage risk-taking in your company?

Examine the answers to these questions quite carefully. You may start to reconsider the effectiveness of your present system and convene a workshop to highlight the issues and to construct an action plan to enable you to improve the rewards strategy of your company. Conducting a detailed SWOT (Strengths, Weaknesses, Opportunities, Threats) analysis may help you to focus on the problems confronting your present strategy. Strengths and weaknesses have an internal focus, whereas opportunities and threats have an external focus.

EXERCISE REVIEW

This exercise may help you concentrate on improvements in the following areas:

- corporate culture;
- attitude surveys;
- rewarding personal effort;
- employee motivation;
- freedom;
- level of customer input;
- commissioning regular research;

■   promoting sales activity;

■   encouraging risk-taking.

collaboration with the people who are working to achieve the targets. One major difficulty in setting targets for creative people is that they may place a *ceiling* on the creative activity of each individual. This means that a collaborative approach is needed to ensure the right balance between actual achievements and the elaborate plans of the strategist.

Many strategic planners are involved in developing new systems of reward and recognition and setting their own trends. The trend is towards a flexible and responsive reward strategy which can adapt to a set of changing business circumstances, a strategy which recognizes the need for personal fulfilment and a desire to achieve in an increasingly competitive working environment.

Certainly the approach of the public sector can assist strategists in

EXERCISE 14: The interdependence of factors in building an effective rewards strategy

The complex nature of many businesses demonstrates the interdependence of many key factors. Let's look at your company.

■   List the main products and services offered by your company:

■   List the products and services that are being developed by your company:

■   List any links your company has with suppliers in terms of research, development or electronic data interchange systems:

■   Examine the interdependencies between all three of these areas of business activity and prioritize discussion points:

■   Comments:

EXERCISE REVIEW

This analysis should enable you to draw some interesting conclusions about the range of interdependencies and linkages within the sphere of activities of your business. This will affect your development of an appropriate reward and recognition strategy.

You can start by asking the right questions of your business and your partners and competitor activities:

■   What approaches to reward strategy are being adopted by your competitors?

■   How are your partners developing future strategic positions?

■   Are there any lessons you can learn from your partners?

■   What is the future direction of interdependency between your company and its partners?

EXERCISE 15: The advantages and disadvantages of approaches to the development of a reward strategy

Let's do an exercise based on your company:

■   Company:

■   Target market:

■   Reward systems:

■   Corporate competencies:

■   Information needs:

■   Reward strategy choice:

Each option will have a series of advantages and disadvantages but you have to make the decision. Which one will you choose and why? The following series of advantages and disadvantages may assist you when making your choice.

Advantages	*Disadvantages*
Commitment	Dilution of control
Spreading of risk	High level of cost
Control	Time for implementation
Management	Long-term commitment required
Quality	Sharing of information
Sharing of risks	Potentially lower productivity
Matching	
Expertise	
Loyalty	

Please outline your initial thinking on your choices:

understanding and developing new approaches that meet the needs of organizations. Many organizations are consistently re-examining their reward and recognition strategy so that they can discover new and exciting ways of increasing corporate creativity.

The majority of reward and recognition systems will focus on the role that is being exercised by the *individual*. In complex organizations a job-evaluation technique can be used to place individuals in a particular role and corporate structure. The job-evaluation technique could be simple and concentrate on non-analytical methods of classification or complex and involve factor comparisons. The difficulty for many companies lies in measuring the worth of each role in the corporate structure. The objective is to arrive at a set of decisions that enable you to compare the information on competitors' reward strategies with the effectiveness of your own strategy.

The approach of the creative company is to pay individuals for their individual creative competencies. The advantages of competency-based reward systems are that you can have a major impact on the corporate culture of the company and alter the strategic direction of the business. This will focus the attention of individuals on acquiring more competencies and utilizing self-development to manage their careers in the organization of the future. The challenge for many companies is to create the appropriate corporate structure and culture to allow the new focus to take place.

CHAPTER SEVEN

Preventing organizational stagnation

The challenge facing your company is how to generate new products and services in a consistent and effective manner, so that long-term business growth can take place. The role of strategist in this instance is to develop policies that can support the business development activities of the company and prevent organizational stagnation. Successful companies are attempting to create a positive mind set for accepting the changes in their organizations that inevitably accompany the drive towards creativity. There is also a move towards the introduction of training and development methods which can encourage creative thinking and leadership at all levels.

The agenda is being set by some of the well-known names from business such as 3M, Microsoft, Kodak and Nissan, who are exploring new and exciting methods of generating creativity within their companies. The agenda is also being set by the organizational functions, which are starting to recognize the impact that people have on the bottom line of their business and responding positively to new ideas on how to manage people. The agenda can be set by the strategic planning function and effectively bypass the Director of Human Resources if he or she does not recognize the opportunity that these changes present for the company. The role of the strategist is not to struggle with other corporate functions in the pursuit of political advantage, but to develop strategic partnerships that can enhance the creativity of their company.

The starting-point for managing the change towards a creative company is based on an understanding of three key factors:

1   The role of the strategic planner is changing.

2   Creativity is required in designing policies to manage people.

3   Internal customer feedback is going to be a necessity in the future.

The people-management policies of the future will be designed with the user in mind. The customers will include business development directors, general manager, product development manager or the marketing planner. Also, the customers could be the operational people in the business, salespeople, customer care personnel, production and manufacturing people or the sales consultant. The external customer must also be considered by the company: training and development provider, external suppliers, potential employees or the corporate investor.

The old-style approach to the management of people emphasized safety and the search for stability. The new style of people management recognizes the need for new thinking and stability through the successful exploitation of the marketplace. The role of the strategist will focus on the ability to intervene, advise and facilitate in the creative process. Key skills will include:

- team-building skills;

- consulting skills to lead strategic change;

- facilitation skills;

- innovation in learning systems;

- advocacy for development opportunities;

- managment of the balance between control and freedom of action;

- design of flexible systems with the user in mind.

Creative strategies for people management

These strategies will not be developed if they are formulated in isolation from the top management team of the company. They require the total support of senior management if they are to be a success. The strategies have to be closely linked to the business development and operational issues of the moment. The important factor is that the people-management strategies have a strong link with the process of strategic planning in the company.

The strategy needs to have the support of the internal and external customers. The internal customer is self-explanatory, but the external customer is any one of the key stakeholders, including trade unions, prospective employees, government, customers, suppliers, bankers, shareholders, managers and the wider community. The working relationships with these stakeholders will act as a springboard into other areas of creative activity:

- *Partnering the customer*: the idea of partnering the customer is an effective method of publicizing the existence of the different benefits that the human resource function can provide for the business development activities of the company.

- *Operational links*: it is necessary to link the activities of the human resource practitioners and the business or product development teams if the function is to gain credibility. One computer-based company where the sales consultants used the facilities of the human resource function did not see how the function actually assisted them in operational terms. This misconception of the role of the human resource management function can damage its image if it is not effectively managed.

- *Response analysis systems*: the lead in the development of human resource management systems has to come from the customers of the function. This requires analytical systems that test the credibility and effectiveness of the initiatives being undertaken by the human resource function.

The response of many strategists may be to do nothing, because a total revision of strategy would be too difficult or time-consuming to contemplate. However, an improvement in four key areas of activity can have a significant effect on any company:

1   Rewards and recognition.

2   Communications.

3   New company employees.

4   Training and development.

These can build the foundations for preventing the organizational stagnation so feared by companies. Policies in these areas can have a direct effect on the momentum of business development in terms of motivation, skills, knowledge and team composition.

Rewards and recognition

These systems have to be clearly linked to the business development activities, research and marketing functions of the business. New thinking is needed to discover a selection of career opportunities that can entice people to join the creative companies of the future and to satisfy their needs for personal development. The hierarchies in many companies are becoming flatter and some companies can envisage a time when the vertical career will no longer exist. This problem can be an opportunity for creative companies because they have the flexibility to adapt to a challenging environment and offer the employee a series of varied and interesting projects.

Reward and recognition systems will need to be flexible and support individuals in their search for a new form of freedom of action. This needs to be tempered with a belief in the individual and a strong element of trust within the company. The new systems need to support risk-taking and be constructive in their criticism when mistakes have been made in the company. The approach to rewards and recognition taken by the public sector has something to teach private-sector organizations because the critical motivational factor is the need for professional recognition and not financial rewards.

For example, a leading computer company has experienced some difficulties in rewarding its business development consultants. The consultants take the view that they are being trained to behave as salespeople. This is a role that they were not recruited for when they joined the company. The view of the consultants is that they need to receive similar remuneration to the sales team if they are to carry out similar work. This situation may cause a series of motivational problems for the company and could have been avoided if the career structure had been more carefully planned and executed.

The career structure of the creative company may have to be geared towards the identification, development and motivation of the entrepreneur. The behaviour and expectations of this person will be different from those of the traditional company employee and will require a career and rewards strategy based on achievement and continuous development.

Communications

Effective communication is fundamental to the success of any new people strategy. The communications system used by a creative company will reinforce strategy and ensure that improved communication becomes an organizational way of life. Any changes in direction or mode of operation will be explained very quickly and this can result in the early dissemination of views from senior management and the effective targeting of information.

The communication methods need to be consistent and must be supported by the actions of the senior management team and the human resource management function. Feedback sessions can be implemented throughout your company which allow discussion on the number, progress and success of new product and service ideas. These sessions can be complemented by focus groups which centre on the problems experienced by people in implementing new products and services. The strategist can act as a facilitator in many of these activities in order to direct thinking towards practical solutions to key implementation issues.

Internal marketing can be adapted to the strategist's role in communicating the people benefits of the creativity strategy. Internal marketing will have two objectives:

1   To communicate the benefits of the new creativity strategy throughout the company.

2   To avoid the political problems that often accompany the introduction of any new strategy.

The components of the internal marketing strategy are:

1   Product: creativity strategy.

2   Price: time.

3   Promotion: message and media.

4   Place: delivery methods.

The product is the creativity strategy. The price equates to the management and employee time used on the successful implementation of the creative strategy. The choice of message is important and should be made carefully by senior management. The choice of delivery method refers to the way in which human resources are managed and which people-management systems are used.

The aim is to make the corporate culture the main distribution channel for the internal marketing of the creativity strategy. The building of links between the marketing function, strategic planning and the human resource management function is crucial to the success of this concept.

The second main objective in using internal marketing is to avoid the negative impact of cultural and political activity. The strategy may be agreed at senior level but a complete acceptance of a new strategic direction for any company is not easy. The strategist needs to work alongside the senior management team to identify the benefits of adopting new policies. This commitment needs to be supported by a high degree of participation in the effective implementation of the strategy.

The need that has been highlighted in my research is for a means of setting company standards of strategy implementation. These standards will have to be set on a clear understanding of the needs of the customer and the influences on customer satisfaction. The formation of information networks assists the communications system and facilitates the movement of ideas throughout the business.

New company employees

The need for experience in information technology, marketing, strategy formulation, languages, team-building and sales is the starting-point. This experience will have to be matched by a series of interesting projects that can support the creative ideas of the individual. In order to enable the creative process to grow and develop, a company will have to construct a stable environment in an unstable business environment.

The new company person may be very different from the traditional longstanding employee of a company. She or he must be able to plan for the unexpected and be suspicious of the safe option that is often the hallmark of the company person. The new person will be secure in the sense that her or his skills and knowledge are in demand by competitors and that she or he is employable elsewhere.

New selection systems will be based on identifying skills and knowledge that can support the following individuals:

- The *focuser* will have a clear focus on the systems of new product development and innovation used by the company. She or he can currently be found in engineering sectors but is not necessarily restricted to that area of activity.

- The *actor* is someone who can take responsibility for her or his own decisions and actions and is particularly useful in developing consultancy business in the information technology sector of the economy.

- The *value adder* is particularly needed in a small business where resources are short and where it is important for every individual to pull her or his weight and accept ultimate responsibility for her or his actions.

- The *challenger* is required in a large multinational which has a very clear idea of its vision and strategy and needs a culture which enables people to challenge the status quo in order to keep the creative process moving.

- The *clear thinker* is desired by the company which has a need for independent drivers within the business who have the confidence to understand what they want to do and the knowledge of the industry and the market to turn ideas into action.

Training and development

Increased activity in the area of training and development in the creative company does not require the wholesale dismantling of the previous systems and procedures. The existing systems will be able to analyse training needs successfully and hopefully develop realistic training plans for each individual in the company. The existing systems need to be reviewed with an objective mind and the present arrangements can build the foundations of a learning culture which can enhance corporate commitment towards creativity. The internal and external customers must be identified and this can only be done through very careful analysis of the prospective customer base.

Auditing systems can play an important role in keeping quality of service high and improving performance in line with the expectations of the development strategy. The audit will focus on the diverse range of customers, markets and the business environment.

The development strategy can be an effective method of securing new business in increasingly difficult and competitive markets. The targets which are set for employees can act as a key motivator. If these targets are supported by a development strategy which recognizes the needs of the frontline creative people and supports their efforts, the credibility of new people-management policies will soar. The development strategy has to recognize that the needs of the business development teams are changing rapidly and that the development specialists need to think quickly and respond dynamically to their needs.

To develop a corporate culture that is able to avoid stagnation the strategist will need to promote a desire among employees to achieve. Inside the creative company there is a strong desire to accept change and welcome the benefits of effective people management. This is often a personal reflection of an individual's aspirations and should be channelled towards the achievement of company goals and not left to lie dormant or to be channelled into outside interests. The strategy developed by your company can assist in the management of the shift towards business development and growth. The human resource management strategy used by a company has a unique position which the marketing strategy or purchasing strategy does not have, that is, the opportunity to tap into an individual's aspirations.

A shift towards business growth is taking place in many companies and the strategist has the opportunity of implementing new thinking in areas of management. If companies are to take advantage of these developments they need to talk honestly to their people about the pressures and difficulties they experience when implementing business development initiatives.

The introduction of new policies is difficult, but if the focus is on maintaining momentum, rewarding and recognizing change, communicating at every level of the process and attracting creative people, your organization can take the first steps towards preventing organizational stagnation and making creativity an organizational way of life.

Many companies are re-examining the contribution made to the business by the management functions in the company. The key challenge for your company will be to harness the knowledge and skills of its people. Information systems will play a major role in the search for competitive advantage. The information will have to focus on a detailed understanding of customers and their needs and on the creative outputs of the company.

Your role could include the key areas outlined in Figure 7.1. The new role will be based on developing relationships that produce ideas, and new methods that drive the creative process in the business and have a direct link to improved corporate performance. The level of productivity expected of people within the organization will be set by customers and how the customers react to new product ideas and service concepts presented to them.

FIGURE 7.1 Your role in the creative process

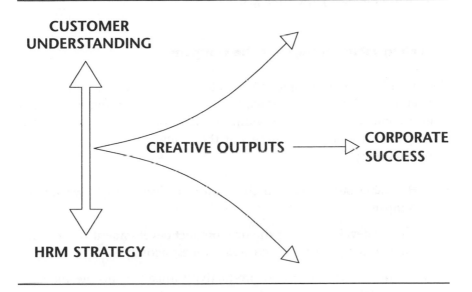

How business growth is achieved in your company

The need to place an emphasis on the business development activities of companies has created a new set of opportunities to use the various people-management techniques that are available. This opportunity is centred on a clear understanding that businesses have to look at markets with fresh eyes and with creativity as the driving force.

Building business partnerships

One method of helping companies to refocus their efforts is to strengthen the links with managers who are at the forefront of the creative process. These managers, or technological specialists, have a clear understanding of their function and personal objectives. The partnership needs to be long term to be effective and the strategist involved must recognize this fact. The opportunity to build long-term relationships will depend on the credibility and relevance the strategist can bring to the table. What is required is a series of achievements or a successful pilot scheme which has a dramatic affect on the progress of the company and a clear view of the contribution made by the strategist.

Providing value throughout the company

You should encourage people to add value to the tasks that they have to fulfil every day. This is quite difficult to achieve, but is feasible with senior management commitment. Providing value throughout the company is an important factor in the success of the creative process. Ask yourself these questions:

- Has value been added to the customer service levels within the company?

- Has the development of the new product development team added value to the process of increased business activity?

- Are the improvements in productivity linked to people management or the business development process?

People initiatives

The people initiatives being implemented in your company can provide an exciting basis for creativity. They may originate in the human resource function, but the actual source of the initiative is irrelevant – what is important is that they flow through the company at a consistent pace. Ask yourself these questions:

- How many development initiatives are taking place?

- Which selection techniques are being used by managers?

- How are promotion and career development decisions linked to business success?

- Is the use of employee communication to underpin creative activity firmly established?

- Is the creativity of company operations reflected in the recruitment process?

- Does the appraisal system reflect the need for creative activity to take place within the company?

- Is there a well-defined and clear strategy concerning creativity and its link to innovation within the company?

Building a competitive advantage in any company is fundamental to the long-term success of the company. Often the competitive advantage of a company is built on a clear set of competencies that are shared and recognized by employees and customers. The competencies that a company develops do not last for ever and the pressure is on management to develop a sustainable competitive advantage.

Creating the freedom to act

The promotion of the freedom and confidence to act is the key activity of the strategist in the creative company. The freedom to act can mean a variety of things to managers and specialists within companies, but fundamentally it means giving people the confidence, beliefs and values to effect a change in behaviour in themselves and their companies.

Company systems and procedures need to be devised with the internal and external customer in mind. Strategic leadership is imperative to the success of the strategy to promote freedom of action within the company. The creative company must tolerate failure and view it as a learning curve that the company has to explore. Trust people to take the the right course of action. Development strategies must be owned by the people who benefit from them. It is important that these people are fully involved in the design of these strategies; this will act as the main driver for motivation. Team-building will enhance the ability of people to act with a degree of freedom. The strategist will have an important role in identifying improvements in team performance.

A key role for the strategist is to manage the changing nature of the management structure within the company. If we look at the different stages of development of the management specialisms we can see quite fundamental changes taking place in their activities.

1   The procurement function is now much more related to the marketing role within companies and links with suppliers and customers are being forged.

2   Marketing is waking up to the benefits of the effective management of people and the implications for the successful development of marketing strategy.

3   Quality managers have been working with strategists in their search for improved levels of quality throughout the company. This is an opportunity to design new systems and procedures to check the standards of creative actions within the company.

4   Business development strategists are aware of the role of effective people in building the future success of the company. The impact that a creative corporate culture can have on the implementation of new business strategies is now widely accepted in management teams.

The old style of functional activity within management teams is now starting to fragment and this requires new thinking in terms of the creative process and how it relates to the performance of management teams. There is a need for an increased level of cross-functional activity.

Taking the creative temperature of the company

One of the first steps to take in searching for a competitive edge through creativity and innovation is to assess the creative actions already taking place in your company. The best method of assessment is to take the creative temperature of the company and build that information into the business and human resource management strategies of the organization. There are several important indicators that can help you assess the creativity of a company and these include:

1   Setting and achieving creative *targets* in terms of new product and service development for the company as a whole.

2   Highlighting individual *achievements* based on creative thinking and examining their impact on the company.

3   Using *competitive benchmarking* procedures to compare the performance of your company against the competition.

4   Monitoring *customer response* levels and the effect of human resource management initiatives when introduced into the company.

When we examine these aspects in more detail we can see the way they might affect the process of taking the creative temperature of the company.

Creative achievements

Creative achievements can take many forms and could include:

- the introduction of a brand new technology into the company by the research departments;

- the design of new management systems for new product and service development;

- the registration of new patents by the company.

The creative achievements of the company require a recognition system to support them and this could be a team or company award or an annual event which serves to highlight creativity within the company.

Best practice – achievement and comparison

This system could be based on the competitive benchmarking approach used by many companies in strategic planning. Criteria could be set by which all achievements are compared and then examined in comparison with competitor's successes.

The criteria will vary depending on the future aims and objectives of the company, which might include:

- setting industry trends;

- developing new approaches to the management of business development units;

- designing new systems to support creative people in their pursuit of new ideas;

- introducing a learning culture which can support creativity and innovation and set the pace for development strategies in your sector.

Monitoring customer response levels

The monitoring of customer response levels is a crucial factor in the achievement of creativity in any company. It is important to identify the internal and external customer as it is very clear that the positive level of feedback received from the customer is the real measure of success or failure.

The information produced by customer feedback systems can act as an important springboard for the success of the human resource function of the creative company.

Starting-point for you

The introduction of people management concepts into the creative company will be a success only if they have the full support of the senior management team. This commitment to leading any major creative activities in the company will help to focus management effort on improving the *creative dynamism* of the company. The challenge for many companies is to provide the support needed throughout their company to enable creativity to take place. This support takes the form of a continuous financial investment backed by a dynamic corporate culture and infused with a process of strategic thinking which can encourage creative management action throughout the company.

The starting-point for achieving strategic creativity through people in your company is the development of a clear definition of creativity by the top team of the company. This clarity of thinking will provide the foundations for the introduction of a creative corporate environment which can provide your company with an opportunity to design a clear business development strategy. These strategic initiatives can work only if they are supported by creative people who are rewarded on their ability to manage risk and have the attributes and skills needed to implement your creative strategy.

Notes

Preface

1 Further guidance for those who wish to develop creative organizations can be found by contacting (in writing) Neil Coade, Coade Management Consultants Limited, c/o International Thomson Publishing, Berkshire House, 168–173 High Holborn, London WC1 7AA.

1 Introduction: strategic creativity

1 For further insight into the required skills and factors for success in developing strategies for creativity, contact Neil Coade (see note 1 of the preface).
2 Public Relations Department, 3M UK, Berkshire, UK.

2 The creative corporate environment

1 CL Fujitsu, Management Development Unit, UK.
2 Leo Burnett, London, UK.
3 Rank Xerox, Quality & Development Units, UK.

3 Innovation and the opportunities for the strategic planner

1 See information provided by the Department of Trade and Industry Innovation Unit, London, UK.
2 Motorola, Business Development Unit, UK.
3 Kings Fund Centre for Health Services Development, London, UK.

4 Selection of creative people

1 Imagination, London, UK.

5 Developing creative people

1 Beefeater (Whitbread Group), Bedfordshire, UK.
2 Motorola External Consultancy Services.

6 Rewarding creative activity

1 Nursing Development Unit: St George's Medical School, London, UK.

Further reading

There are many books which are relevant to those seeking to develop their skills in strategic creativity.

These are some of my recommendations.

Semler, R. (1993) *Maverick*, Century.
Pearson, G. (1992) *The Competitive Organisation*, McGraw Hill.
Cooper, R. (1988) *Winning at New Products*, Kogan Page.
Dussauge, P., Hart, S. and Ramanantsoa, B. (1992) *Strategic Technology Management*, Wiley.
Thorne, P. (1992) *Organising Genius*, Blackwell.
Burns, T. and Stalker, G. M. (1994) *The Management of Innovation*, Tavistock.
Twiss, B. (1987) *Managing Technological Innovation*, Pitman.
Coade, N. (1997) *Managing International Business*, International Thomson Business Press.
Hippel, V. (1988) *Sources of Innovation*, Oxford University Press.
Henry & Walker (1991) *Managing Innovation*, Sage.
Urban, G. L. and Hauser, G. R. (1993) *Design and Marketing of New Products*, Prentice Hall.
Pinchot, G. (1985) *Intrapreneuring*, Harper & Row.

Index